THE GLOW UP GUIDE

ELEGANTLY SIPPING YOUR WAY TO SUCCESS

SANA GROVER

notionpress.com

INDIA · SINGAPORE · MALAYSIA

ISBN 979-8-88975-914-0

Dedicated to the most elegant lady I know,
my mom.

Table of Contents

Chapter 1

Why Did I Buy This Book?

You might find yourself asking, "Why did I buy this book?"

To transform our lives (and have an *actual* glow-up), a good starting point is 'etiquette'.

Take a minute and think about the rudest thing someone has ever done to you. For me, I remember I was walking on the streets of New York City with my grandma, who was naturally a little slow walker because of her recent knee operation.

New York, being New York, has a culture where everyone is in a rush, constantly moving to the next place (with a coffee tumbler in their hand).

Although my grandma and I were walking on the side of the walkway, a lady overtook us, turned around and asked us to walk faster.

It wasn't really a big deal, but it's something that stuck in my mind forever.

A very talented friend of mine was told in school by her accountancy teacher that she'll never amount to anything in life, just because accountancy wasn't her cup of tea. To date, she feels underconfident trying to navigate through the balance sheets of her very well-performing business.

Reflect on the rudest thing someone has done. It could be someone excluding you from a party, spreading rumours, making you feel stupid for the sake of looking cool, pretending not to know you, going through your diary, or cancelling plans at the last minute only to go out with their boyfriend.

Here's the thing — more often than not, we don't realise how our words and actions impact others. Etiquette is simply having consideration for the feelings of others. The purpose of manners is to make people feel comfortable.

However, as with anything, an excess can make people feel uncomfortable. This handbook will help you find the sweet spot!

In my family, we've always had this rule to never hang up the phone without saying bye to each other. My grandma made sure everyone's privacy was respected, even the children's. We all knock on doors before entering, avoid going through each other's things and ask before borrowing clothes or accessories. But we are far from the ideal family and like everyone else, we do make mistakes. What's important is we apologise if mistakes are made and make efforts to be nice and not repeat it.

Humans were hunter-gatherers and ate on the go. Around 9000 BC, people started eating together, communally. This involved rituals, and these rituals passed from generation to generation. Anything we can find about etiquette first came around 2500 BC, containing all sorts of advice for getting along with others and moving ahead in society. Over the years, manners continued to develop.

Today, etiquette is alive, it's happening now and it's constantly changing as society evolves. In Victorian times, men and women used to curtsy or bow upon being introduced and used to get in and out of carriages. In today's day and age, of course, we draw from guidelines already put in place, but we also have newer ways of living, a different kind of lifestyle involving mobile phones and social media. As our lifestyles evolve, so does etiquette.

While this book serves as a guide to modern-day etiquette, etiquette and manners are also context-sensitive. Social guidelines differ across cultures and within subcultures. Most Asian households ask for shoes to be kept outside the house, whereas in Western countries, it's absolutely okay to bring the shoes in.

It also requires constant adjustment. For instance, at restaurants guests never pay, but what if the guest insists?

Or when the cheque is handed over to the man, does the woman never pay?

We'll uncover all of this in the upcoming sections of this book.

Ready, ladies?

Chapter 2

There's Never a Second Chance for a First Impression

Remember how in school we were taught to have groomed nails, properly done hair and taught good manners? It's never too early to start being concerned about your appearance – first impressions are everything.

More than anything, physical appearance helps boost self-confidence and self-esteem. You feel reassured when other people admit and prefer to associate with you. In certain professions, it makes a huge difference. Consider a model or a salesperson – anyone who is groomed well gets noticed quicker than others.

A pleasant person is nice to interact with. People like to relax in the presence of beautiful things and those with an aesthetic sense admire such people.

A smart, well-dressed politician can draw the attention of the masses, of course, he or she has to be a person of substance, but think of John F Kennedy – he was known for his looks besides being a great politician. Looks elevated his public image.

It's as simple as that.

Statistics show that

55% of initial attention focuses on appearance,

and 38% focus on behaviour.

This leaves only 7% of attention to hear what is being said.

So how do you make a great first impression?

Be on time. Imagine inviting someone for lunch at 2 pm and they arrive 15 minutes late. You have another meeting scheduled at 3.45 pm. Running late is a huge turn-off, and no one wants to be at the receiving end of it. Arriving a tad bit early is never looked down upon, but arriving late can be a major deal-breaker.

For social occasions and gatherings, being 10 minutes late is okay.

For one-to-ones, reach 5 minutes early.

Do your homework. If it's an interview you're going for, the first thing you need to do is have your research done. Now apply this habit while meeting anyone for the first time. You should know something about them; even a little bit is okay.

Remember the scene in The Devil Wears Prada, where Emily forgets the name of the Ambassador and Andrea jumps to

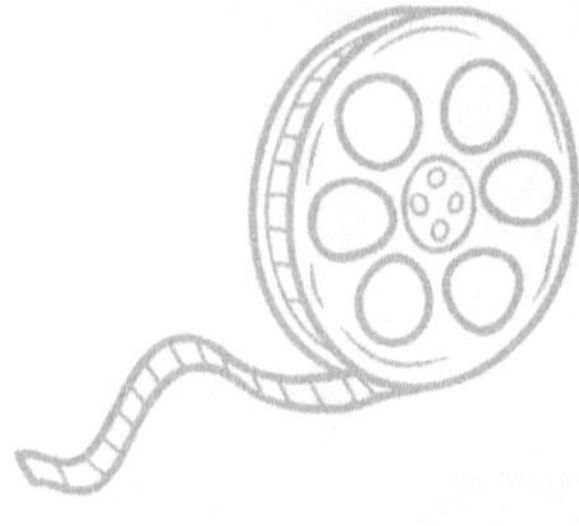

Miranda Priestley's rescue, telling her the lady with the ambassador was not his wife, but the lady he left his wife for? See how crucial it was for Miranda to recognise everyone at the party. Imagine if she asked if that was his wife. Awkward!

Put your phone away. Not on the table, not the other way around. Simply tuck it away. I was once on a date with someone who would always get work calls, even on a weekend. It was fine a couple of times until it started bothering me. If it bothers you too, make a mental note to never do this to anyone. Sometimes meet-ups can get boring and you may feel like checking the number of likes your latest Instagram post got but don't give in. It's not only offensive but you're already making a poor first impression of yourself.

Be open. Do you want to keep the ball rolling? Be open and optimistic. No one likes someone who's cancelling out everything the other one has to say. Encourage people to speak and share more. Do a subtle head nod; it always helps! Trust me, when you do this, you might come across as one of the best people that person has ever met in their entire life.

Give people space. Someone invading your personal space can feel quite unwanted, awkward and in all honesty, uncomfortable. In India, we have a collectivistic culture; we take pride in being together and in having strong ties with friends and family, and we may even compromise on our own happiness and time if it means others are happy, and that's great! But in the middle of that, sometimes we forget the concept of space. Most of us who grow up watching Western content like movies, shows or even social media channels, have had constant exposure to Western society and subconsciously we develop individualistic traits. How close you stand to someone, do you hug or shake hands, do you go ahead and kiss on the cheek – all depends on your equation with them, but a good idea is to respect their personal space as and when you can, and never be too touchy – please.

And finally, **look for common ground**. I have distant cousins who visit us once in five years, and there is a huge age gap between us. In all honesty, any interaction with them is terrible! (I pray they're not reading this).

As much as I hate it, I don't wish anything along the same lines happens to you. Thus, when you think of making a great first impression, think of hobbies or interests you both share. Maybe you're following your cousin on Instagram and know they like painting or stitching. It's always something you can bring up.

Chapter 3

Introducing, Meeting & Greeting Like a Princess

Meetings are accidental, introductions are created.

We meet people all the time, socially and professionally but anyone who is able to introduce themselves smartly stands out. It's just a very useful skill to have. It's an art, and all good artists have nailed this skill, but only a great artist knows the core principles of greetings and introductions.

True honour is recognised by the name spoken first.

Courtesy gives honour to those who are :

- Female
- Older
- Higher ranking
- Distinguished
- Travelled the farthest

Let's say your grandmother meets your friend for the first time at your birthday party. How do you introduce them to each other?

The correct way to do it is:

"Nani, I'd like to introduce you to Surina."

When you say their names, make sure you look at them. It creates a sense of warmth and emotional connection.

You must also make sure the introductions are balanced. If it is a business dinner and you introduce your boss X to a potential client Y, you say:

"Y, I'd like to introduce you to X, X this is Y…."

Then you follow that with a line or two about both parties.

This makes sure the communication is clear, everyone has context and your introduction is balanced.

Voila, you've learnt it!

If, as a host, your event is in Delhi, and you have a friend who travelled from Mumbai, when you introduce them to another friend who is from Delhi, make sure you first say the name of the person who travelled the farthest.

Introducing Yourself

HELLO!
ALOHA!
BONJOUR
HOLA

Let's say you just joined university and don't know who's who. It's your first day, and you know the right thing to do is to go introduce yourself to others, but shyness gets the best of you.

There's a correct way to introduce yourself. Once you learn it, you'll never have to worry about messing up ever again.

Step 1: Offer a handshake.

Step 2: Give your name.

"Hey, I'm Jagriti. I just joined BA Psychology and wanted to come say hello."

That's it. It's a simple one-liner. Congratulations, this one line can create lifelong friendships and give you a great support system forever.

At this point, the other person is ideally supposed to do the same and introduce themselves. When they do, make sure you remember their name correctly.

When I went to London, I was very bad with names, especially ones that weren't Indian. Pronunciations were difficult to ace, let alone spellings. A trick that worked really well was to repeat the name to myself a couple of times after the introduction was done.

In case you misunderstand the name, simply say,

"Sorry, I didn't get it, could you repeat that for me?"

Repeat it back to the person and wait for them to say a yes or give a head nod.

Understanding Titles

Anyone who is groomed well understands the importance of titles.

Unless it's a very personal, intimate and casual setting, titles are of utmost importance. In business settings, they help set context regarding the other person's position.

My grandfather was in the Indian Army and retired as a Colonel. Anyone from the military would know how much time and hard work goes into going up the ranks. Unfortunately, our schooling system doesn't teach us much about this.

Another fun fact about my grandpa: he loves going to the bank. It's as if he has made friends with people from the bank. Initially, the staff didn't know what Colonel meant or how to read it out. While this didn't bother Nanu, it can seem rude to others. To save yourself from the horror, learn the basic titles:

Mr.

Regardless of whether a man is married or not, the title 'Mr.' is used before his last name or full name. It's simply pronounced as Mister.

Master is used for younger boys, although there is no separate abbreviation.

Ms.

Whether a woman is married or not, the title 'Ms.' is used before her last name or full name.

Mrs.

A married female is addressed as Mrs. before her last name or full name.

Missus is referred to as Mrs.

Miss

An unmarried female is addressed as Miss before her full name.

Mx.

Mx is a gender-neutral term and is now being widely accepted. It is pronounced as Mix.

Let's say you are unclear about the title a lady uses, just ask. Avoid going wrong with titles because a lot of people can find it personally offensive, especially if the lady has separated from her partner and you refer to her as Mrs.

It's all in the details.

For the military, here are the ranks we follow in India.

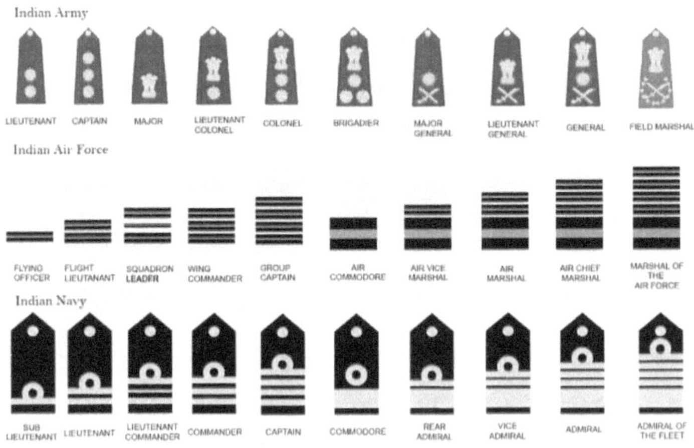

Chapter 4

To Shake Hands or Not to Shake Hands?

Networking and socialising can get you places, but it's difficult to go out there and talk about yourself. I get it, introducing yourself is hard as it is, how are you supposed to go and talk all about your job, your passion projects, your family, the list goes on and on…

Here's the secret:

Assume the burden of other people's discomfort.

Most people hate networking and avoid such events because they're socially difficult, but once you learn how to navigate through the discomfort and present yourself, not only would you carry yourself gracefully, but you'd also be putting others at ease.

My college would often organise placement fairs, which I never attended because I hated talking about my achievements until I learnt the correct way to do it. It's what sets the amateurs apart from the people who know what they're doing and do it successfully.

When you enter a room, pause and spot key people. As you approach them, maintain great posture and open body language. You don't want to cross your arms and meet them. Look and feel approachable. If the occasion calls for a smile, go ahead and do that. If not, it's okay to put on your serious face. Although, I'd say a gentle smile never hurt anybody. Before you start mingling, greet the hostess first and then circulate with handshakes and a self-introduction.

Here are a few tips to keep in mind while networking:

- **Drinks in your right.** Most social networking events have drinks, but avoid drinking too much unless you want to be a total hot mess. When you take a drink, hold it in your left hand so you can always keep your right hand free for handshakes.

- **Avoid controversial topics.** No one likes discussing politics or religion socially. Someone can have entirely opposing views and feel offended. The idea is to always make others feel comfortable in your presence.
- **Be culturally sensitive in your interactions.** Nothing derogatory, even as a joke.
- **Saying goodbye.** When you leave a party or a formal event, always say goodbye to the host or hostess. It's just rude not to.

- **Saying thanks.** Send a quick 'thank you' message to the host after the event. You might even want to mention something that you particularly liked, like the food or the decor. It shows you were invested, you cared and appreciated the details.

Reading the room *is a skill you acquire with time. Here are a few tricks I've picked up over the years that might help you:*

- **Avoid groups of two** since they might be in deep conversation and you don't want to seem intrusive.
- **Pay attention to people's feet.** Without sounding like a creep, when people stand with their feet open, they're more likely to welcome another person to the group to talk to. If their feet are joined and facing the person they are talking to, they are really invested in the conversation.
- **As the host** of a networking event, it is your duty to keep the environment open and conversations going. People should feel at ease and be able to talk freely.

"Be a farmer, never a hunter."

Simply put, build relationships. Networking is not just about gathering business cards or adding people on LinkedIn and calling them only when you need their help. Pay attention to what people express about themselves, their family or their friends. Nurture your relationships.

Back in college, my professor once told me his daughter wanted to start a YouTube channel. A few days later, I came across an article on ways to grow on YouTube based on the current algorithm. I mailed it to him with a little note expressing how when I came across the article, I remembered him mentioning his daughter's interest and thought she could benefit from reading it.

This one act of building a relationship helped more than any academic qualification could.

Even taking out 10 minutes in the entire day and texting someone to check up on them or catch up can help you build relationships for life. It's simple if you let it be simple.

Let's talk handshakes.

While on the surface, a handshake may seem as simple as, well, just a handshake, there are hidden negotiation techniques in handshakes that body language experts spent years understanding.

So, what's in a handshake?

- **An equal handshake** means you and the other person are on the same page mentally. You're both equals. This is an ideal case scenario.
- When someone **cups your hand**, it simply goes to say, "Don't worry, I'll take care."
- When someone's **hand is on top of yours**, it says I'm superior to you.
- A **lousy handshake** can mean weakness and shows that you're easy to control.
- And then we have **the bone-crusher.** No one likes this person and I, for one, take off all my rings before I shake hands with this person. They simply cannot do a gentle handshake, hence the name 'bone-crusher.' This usually goes to say, "I'm superior to you and I want you to know it."

Chapter 5

Diplomacy – But Make it Verbal

We use language to form and transform social bonds. What we mean by 'communication' extends beyond just 'sending and receiving messages.'

Our daily conversations typically revolve around mundane topics like "What time are you arriving home for dinner?" or "Whose turn is it to pay the bills?"

We text each other reminders like "Don't forget to pick up dog food on the way home" and "It's your time to take the dog out" (if you have not guessed, a lot of the messages in my house are about my dog, Candy).

When things go wrong, we often attribute it to a failure in communication or say that there was a 'miscommunication.'

Our identities and the identities of our personal and familial connections are affected, reflected and changed by both happy and negative experiences.

Let me explain what I mean. When and how did these connections form? Consider your most recent experience of making a new friend or welcoming a new family member into your life. These connections were shaped by the words and actions exchanged between you and the other person, or what we call verbal and non-verbal communication.

In some cases, connections become obvious and easy to understand, but sometimes partnerships grow through testing circumstances, and their eventual health is uncertain. The ways in which we talk to one another pave the way for successful beginnings, successful issue-solving, and successful evolution in our relationships.

Relationships grow, change and evolve because of communication. The more we talk, the more we learn about ourselves and the world, and the more we grow and develop as people. Consider how your interpersonal communication skills at home, in the workplace, with friends, and in the community have developed over the years.

What you say really does make a difference.

Here are a few things every elegant lady keeps in mind while communicating:

- The **words you pick and how they are received and perceived** make up the verbal part of communication.
- The message's **reception is just as crucial as its transmission**.
- Remember that your **body language, tone of voice and facial expressions**, among other non-verbal cues, are crucial to conveying the intended message effectively when speaking with others.
- The success of every verbal exchange may be improved by paying **attention to detail, your level of composure, politeness** and adherence to a few simple standards of conduct.

When you first meet someone, you form an opinion of them based on their physical appearance, their voice and demeanour, and whatever rumours or gossip you may have heard about them. You may use this first impression to shape your subsequent interactions.

When you listen to them talk, for instance, you make assumptions about who they are, where they came from, and how much you can expect them to know. Your response might shift in light of this.

For instance, you could opt to simplify your language in response to a foreign accent. Maybe you'll also come to terms with the fact that you'll have to pay more attention in order to pick up on what they're saying.

You might even find yourself slightly modifying your accent to help the other person understand you better (trust me, this is more common than it seems, and it's not a bad thing).

Sometimes we need to say things that might not necessarily be the nicest. Tough situations arise, even in the life of a very elegant lady, and that's where verbal diplomacy helps.

Let's say you're in a group project and your teammate messed up the part they were responsible for. This is always a tricky situation.

Instead of saying, "This isn't good, I don't like it,"

say "I think we can work on this a bit better. Would you like me to help?"

Instead of saying "No, it's not possible,"

say, "I'm afraid this won't be possible, but we can do this (with an alternative)."

A Lady in Training Must Know How to Talk to the Masses

The **words you pick**, the **way you pronounce** them, and the **use of non-verbal cues** are the three key components of effective public speaking. Your audience's reception and interpretation of your message are affected by all of these factors.

- Your word choice has an impact, so give it some thought. Even when talking about the same thing, various contexts will call for distinct terminology. What you may say to a close colleague, for instance, and what you could say at a large conference, on the same topic, will be quite different. Subtleties, remember.

- The tone of voice and speech rate are examples of how you communicate. They convey how invested you are in the topic, how concerned you are about their reply, and so on.

- The ability to listen attentively is rarer than we think it is. When we talk to someone, we spend a lot more time planning what we're going to say than we do actually listening to what the other person is saying.

- Strong communication and relationship building begin with attentive listening. You may improve your listening skills in several ways:

- Keep in mind the overarching theme that the speaker is trying to convey. Grasp both the big picture of what they're getting at and the finer points of the language they're using.

- If possible, steer clear of interruptions. If there is a lot of ambient noise, for instance, just suggest moving the conversation elsewhere.

- Don't interrupt someone who's talking to you by formulating a question. It's annoying when someone does it while we talk, let's not make it difficult for others.

- Avoid assuming negative characteristics about the speaker. Keep your biases about the speaker's gender, race, accent, socioeconomic status, looks, or clothing out of the way.

It's Time to Say Goodbye

The way a discussion is left open or concluded can have a significant impact on how it is remembered. I love meeting my mom's cousin simply because of how she makes me feel while we talk. It's an art, girls.

When it comes to concluding, you can finish a discussion in several ways, both verbally and non-verbally.

Phrases like "Thank you very much, that's really helpful," might serve as a verbal signal. Conclusions can be drawn non-verbally by actions such as avoiding eye contact, rising, turning away, checking the time, or putting down a book or notepad. These non-verbal cues let the recipient know that you want to close the conversation.

Even while many people use a combination of these methods, non-verbal cues, especially when sent directly to the recipient's eyes, are typically the first to be employed.

Make sure there is time for winding up before ending a conversation to give the other person a chance to 'round out' what they were saying. Any plans should be made before an encounter ends.

Chapter 6

Mastering the Art of Dialogue

Do you recall Bollywood legend Amitabh Bachchan's booming baritone? He became known in the 1970s as the 'angry young man,' thanks to his tone of voice and intense speech.

On the other hand, Barack Obama's warm and comforting voice helped him become the president of the United States. The tone of one's voice is a powerful instrument in public speaking and a crucial aspect of effective communication.

Just what does 'tone of voice' entail?

When describing a person's tone of voice, the phrase "the way a person talks to someone" is sometimes used. This refers to the tone and volume of your speaking voice. The chance of your message being misunderstood or overlooked increases if you don't do it properly. Humour is an excellent example of a tone. Genuine humour endears your audience to you and leaves them feeling hopeful and optimistic.

According to the ancient Greek philosopher Aristotle, there are three ways to influence someone else: reason, emotion and character. The communication style of the great Greek orators was built on a problem–solution framework, and it was used to persuade audiences. In nearly every case, this led to the expected outcomes.

A monotone voice might be uninteresting and turn off listeners. A good speaker should flawlessly adjust their tone to fit social and professional contexts. Here are some examples of different tones:

- **Encouragement-Inducing Tone of Voice.** A positive tone keeps the speaker interested and gives them energy for both their personal and professional life.
- **Vocal Tone that Informs.** How come certain educators manage to make such a deep impact on their students' lives? Their vocal tone is a contributing factor. Knowledge is increased, information is given, and personal development is inspired by a tone of voice that is instructive.
- **A Soft, Gentle Voice.** Intimate interactions typically take place in a soft tone. It's a connection builder. It's a way to show compassion and kindness in trying situations.
- **Using Humour.** There's nothing a bit of humour can't solve. Use entertaining tales or quotes to keep the tone light and upbeat during your speech.

Have you ever noticed different cultures have different ways of speaking?

In South Asian cultures, we complete our sentence and then the other person responds with a complete sentence as well.

In Japanese culture, between dialogues, there is a slight gap to make sure the listener has processed what the speaker just said.

In France, there's a lot of overlap between the dialogues, but this is not considered rude, it's just socially acceptable.

It's important that we learn the subtleties of the places we travel to better understand how the culture works. Always be well-informed and appreciative of local cultures.

Chapter 7

Formal and Informal Tone

Different types of writing, such as those found in the academic world, the media, and the corporate world, all have certain goals and styles.

I once had to write a letter (who does that in today's day and age!?) to the police station about a cybercrime case, and while I had learnt letter writing for almost ten years of my school life, I was blank when I held the pen.

Formal writing must be error-free in terms of grammar, spelling, punctuation and use. Some letters, such as those in which you lodge a formal complaint (ahem), may call for a more official tone.

- In general, lengthier sentences are more proper for formal writing. The overall approach to formal writing is more organised, with defined introductions, body paragraphs and conclusions. Writing for formal purposes is usually well-thought-out, updated and evaluated several times to ensure clarity and completeness.

- Avoid shortening phrases and use whole words instead. Using contractions to shorten words is discouraged in formal writing. You just wouldn't end your letter to the police station with an 'XOXO.'

- First uses of acronyms should often be written out in full.
- Keep in mind to use straightforward words and sentences. If you use a bunch of big words wrongly, you won't sound any smarter than you already are.
- Extremely formal language is unlikely to upset anyone, but it is surely possible to cause offence by coming across as overly casual.

Your 'XOXO' moment may happen when you're writing to a friend (or simply DMing them).

- Dialects and jargon of common usage.
- Informal writing, like spoken language, features shorter sentence lengths and paragraphs. This holds truer than ever before for writers putting their words out there in cyberspace.
- Words may be condensed or truncated in casual writing just as they are in the spoken language.

So which one is better?

A more formal tone in writing is neither 'better' nor 'worse' than a more conversational tone. Neither is always inappropriate. Their functions are very distinct from one another, so be mindful of picking the right format for the job.

Writing for business or official purposes usually calls for a more formal tone. However, if you are writing to someone you know in person, you may be allowed to employ a more casual manner.

Emails also adopt a more casual tone than traditional paper correspondence. However, this is beginning to change as more businesses go to email as their primary method of communication. Therefore, you should not use speech-to-text (I used to do this all the time) or excessive informality.

Chapter 8

A Lady in the Digital World

Email and Texting Etiquette

Many people believe letter writing to be a dying art. Nobody talks to anyone nowadays unless it's via email or DM. This should show that everyone is conversant with email composition, but the data says otherwise.

If you do not include the correct individuals or strike the wrong tone, everyone will be left wondering what went wrong.

- The first thing to consider when sending an email is to whom you should send it, and whether you should use the 'To,' 'Cc,' or 'Bcc' lines.

TO

'To' shows the intended reader or the person being prompted to take some sort of action. In the case of a single recipient, the word 'To' should always be used.

CC

Those who should be copied on an email, but need not respond directly to the message are 'cc'd.' This is standard practice when sending an email to someone and you want them to know that it has been sent. This person (or people) may be your manager, or they could be a group: for instance, if you have consented to send an email on behalf of a club or organisation, and you want the committee to know that you have done so, and what you said, you would 'cc' them in.

BCC

Use blind carbon copy (Bcc) when you want someone to view the email but don't want the sender or recipients to be publicly identified. It's also used in situations when it's important to keep people's email addresses private, such as on a club or society mailing list. Email recipients who have been bcc'd are prevented from replying to all.

Nothing is more annoying that a chain of mails that you don't need in your inbox simply because everyone started abusing the 'reply all' feature. Please give some thought to whether you really need to respond to an email you receive, and whether you really need to 'reply to everyone' (meaning that your response will be sent to everyone in the 'To' or 'Cc' list for the email).

- **The Topic of the Email.** No one can handle a flood of emails without any way to sort them. The topic at hand is the process by which recipients choose which ones to view right away, later, or not at all. Put the gist of your message in the subject line. Indicate in the subject line if your message is time-sensitive or if it's merely informative.

DO NOT use this in an inappropriate way. If you do this, the people you're trying to reach will be considerably less likely to pay attention to any 'urgent' emails you send them in the future, rendering this tactic useless even in the face of dire necessity (basically urgent mails don't include chit-chat time with your work bestie).

- **Beginning an email** with a greeting like 'Dear [Name]' or 'Hi [Name]' is widely seen as proper practice. If you don't know the person you're writing to, it's best to use the more formal 'Dear.'
- **Thanking the sender** for their email and supplying added context, such as, "Thank you for your email concerning [topic]," is important when replying to emails from others. Even if you're responding right away, there's no telling when they'll really see it; they might already have fifty emails in their inbox.
- **Signing out** with a kind farewell like 'Best wishes' or 'Kind regards' is also appreciated and can help foster future ties. This also

acts as a visual indicator to the receiver that the email has been read in its entirety. If you add a comma after the initial greeting (Dear/Hello/Good Morning), add a comma after your 'Kind Regards' as well.

Communication Style and Tone. Unless Siri learns to read and convey our facial expressions while we type out an email (which is 99% of the time going to be a straight face with zero expression), the recipient of an email does not have the benefit of the sender's body language, facial expression or tone of voice in deciphering the intended meaning of the message. As a result, people tend to accept others at their word. To prevent upsetting others, it is crucial to use the proper tone and words.

When sending an email, especially one of a formal or professional nature, NEVER use sarcasm or try to make a joke. It's not a good idea to use emoticons here since they might cause offence.

The Final Signature. It is proper etiquette to sign off emails with enough information for the receiver to recognise you and reply to you.

For more casual communication, just your first name is OK. If your first name is common and/or your email address holds obscure symbols, you may need more than the minimum.

Any time you communicate with a school, college or university, a doctor or other health service provider or an employer through email, consider it a business email and sign off with your full name.

These days, a lot of techs can automatically sign off on your emails with a custom signature. "Sent from my iPhone" or "Sent from Windows Mail" are two such phrases. Please remove this, it just doesn't look professional.

Email signatures from the company itself are also common practice. Even if you or your company already has one of these in place, you may want to consider starting one for yourself.

Okay, but can we talk about the more casual (aka socially acceptable way of communicating)?

When I was in London doing my Masters, my Nani would send me good morning quotes on WhatsApp. It's safe to say I had a good laugh looking at some of them, but more importantly, I realised texting has become such a huge practice between people of all age groups, and might even have replaced the more conventional phone calls.

Texting is quick and easy, but it also has its drawbacks. Without proper context, words can be taken the wrong way, messages can be left unfinished and social norms can be broken without your knowledge.

- Always make sure that your text messages reflect the image of yourself that you want to convey. When texting with co-workers, clients, or potential customers, you should use an altogether different tone than when texting with friends.

- Before pressing the 'send' button, be sure your message makes sense on its own.

- One's expectation of a prompt response from you after receiving a text message is much higher. Unless you can't, try to answer as soon as possible; otherwise, your silence might be taken as a sign that you don't care. If you are delayed in responding, please express regret as soon as possible.

- Only use emojis and symbols when essential (*joined hands **please** emoji*). There are instances when a smiley face is proper in a text message, and therefore they included them. However, you should be aware of the contexts in which emojis are inappropriate. When speaking on a professional level, for instance, the use of emoticons such as smiling faces is frowned upon. Keep your heartfelt emoticons for direct communication. If in doubt, don't include them.

- Responding to a two-word SMS with many pages may be seen as annoying. Short texts are usually a sign that the sender is in a rush, does not have much time, or requires an immediate answer. Please pick up the phone or arrange a face-to-face meeting if you need to supply a lengthy explanation.

- Do not bombard someone with messages before you've had a chance to hear back from them. Simply put, texting is just like talking or writing. Recognise when the other person wants to end the conversation through text and don't persist or harass them with questions like 'Are you still there?' or 'Why aren't you responding?'

Chapter 9

Small Talk, Big Networks

Making conversation is more difficult than it seems. Anybody who has been forced to chat about recent news events at a wedding reception or cocktail party will agree. It's not always easy to strike up a conversation with a complete stranger. However, there is a technique to it that can be learnt.

'You don't have to be great; just kind.'

- **Show up with your doubts.** Keep a few intriguing queries in your back pocket for those times when you need a conversation starter on the move.

- **Try to think of at least a couple of topics to discuss** on the way to the party in case the discussion dies down. If you have met the host previously, it is polite to bring up a topic of conversation related to the host's interests or activities, such as the host's love of skiing or a common charity you both support.

- **Add some flair to your reply.** Don't be vague. Look, most of us don't like small talks, but in certain social situations, you have to. And it's never as bad as it seems. You shouldn't, for instance, respond to a query about your occupation with a single word like 'fine,' leaving the other person to fend for themselves in terms of follow-up inquiries.

- **People love to talk about themselves,** so learn to be a good listener. My friend was in the middle of an ugly break-up recently, and I didn't know what to say to her. All I did was listen (for like, hours and hours and hours…), and it worked. She felt much better. Networking requires you to think of interesting things to inquire about, such as favourite pastimes or vacation spots. It is not necessary to ask very precise inquiries. Just say, 'Get me caught up.'

- **Green topics** are absolute safe zones – if you make a remark on the atmosphere, such as the music, the flowers, or the length of the food line, and the other person agrees with you, it's a good sign that they want to strike up a conversation. Another situation-specific, certain question is "How do you know the host?" With green topics, usually, there is no room for any confrontation or discomfort.

Yellow topics include dicey questions like "Where did you go on vacation?" We may not realise, but the other person might not want to share where they went, since that also relates to how much they spent on vacation. If there is a significant economic difference between the two, the other person might not want to make you feel uncomfortable by mentioning how economic or lavish of a vacation it was. Remember, you never want to make the other person uncomfortable, and sometimes, the other

person may want to avoid such topics simply because they don't want us to feel awkward (even if you are unbothered about their totally lavish vacation).

We can do without this information, so avoid the slippery slopes.

Red topics include politics, religion and money, and as tempting as they are, *just don't*. Save those for when you meet ministers and dignitaries, not regular people just wanting to know more about you. And please never ask someone how much they make. If someone asks about your salary, just laugh it off. I usually say, *"Oh, it's never enough."*

- **When there is silence, don't freak out.** Silences aren't as long as you may assume. It's important to keep in mind that the other person may require some time to think about what you've said. Consider the pause as a new beginning.
- **Don't prevent the other person from leaving** if you can tell they're desperate to get away.

If you meet someone who is really self-absorbed (and trust me, there are quite a few), it's best to politely withdraw from the conversation.

You can use the word **need** in this situation: "I need to grab some food; I haven't eaten all day." It's also quite okay to exit by saying you'd like to refill your drink, visit the toilet, catch up with a buddy who just arrived, or make sure your partner is okay.

Don't leave without mentioning something pleasant about the conversation, like "It was great talking to you about London" or "I can't wait to hear everything about your vacation to Hawaii once you return!"

I have a school friend who loves to talk only about her boyfriend. While all of us are happy for her, it can be really (like, really) annoying at times. So how do we solve the issue? We've made internal group signs to get out of such a sticky situation.

Our 'rescue me' sign is three coughs. Do this and another friend would be there to ask you to attend an *important call on her phone*.

Get your acting skills on, and voila!

Chapter 10

Get Your Party Hat On

Sending and Receiving Invites

A lady knows how to party. But more importantly, she knows how to host the *party of the year!*

Your social life will truly take off as you attend parties and even host gatherings for people. Being a good host or hostess is vital, but so is being a gracious guest. Others will be more likely to invite you again if you make them happy, as they did. If you're a good host or hostess, guests will accept your invitations and in fact, be excited to attend.

Sending Invites

It is polite to send invitations while hosting a party. People's schedules are often busy; you must give your friends advance notice if you want them to attend.

For less formal occasions, invites can be bought, made, or even sent via text message. However, remember to give your visitors at least three weeks' notice, particularly during busy periods like Diwali and summer vacations.

51

So what do you put on an invite?

- Your name
- The event's date, time, and location
- Any requests or instructions
- When you need to know if they're coming, set an RSVP date (this also helps decide how many people you have to cater for food). RSVP is an abbreviation of the French phrase "Répondez s'il vous plaît," meaning please respond.

- Allergies to meats, nuts and certain vegetables are common. Unless you want a messy hospital situation after your party, asking about dietary preferences is always important. It also shows the invitees that you care. Remember, the subtleties, ladies.
- Make sure to distribute invitations outside of school or the office if you aren't inviting everyone in your class or team to avoid offending anyone (that includes the girl you hate – been there, done that).

We request the pleasure of your company to celebrate Diwali

On

Saturday, 22nd October (date)

7 pm Onwards (time)

XYZ Street, 123909 (location)

RSVP: 17th October (contact number)

Put on your dancing shoes and bring your favourite booze.

Please let us know any dietary preferences.

Receiving Invites

- Say 'thank you' when you receive an invitation.
- The host would want to know whether you can make it; therefore, they use this small code 'RSVP' that has been around for a long time. Please respond as soon as possible, preferably within a day or two of receiving the invitation, and no later than the RSVP deadline specified.
- You must never ask the host to change the date of the event if you are busy on the date they have planned.

A lady never tries so hard to make herself the centre of attention.

- If you find out at the last minute that you will not be able to attend a party you had agreed to attend, try to notify the host, apologise for having to cancel, and provide a brief explanation of the problem.
- If you must buy a gift, ask the recipient if there is anything they would want, and allow yourself time to make the purchase, wrap the gift and write a message.

What do I say in response?

Please respond to the invitation as specified:

- Your RSVP, if you don't have a response card, should be a letter/email (in case of formal) or text (in case of informal invites) to the host.
- Please complete the included response card and give it in the postmarked envelope by the due date.
- Please call the listed number to confirm your attendance.
- You can electronically accept or refuse the invitation by email.
- **Please only respond if you are unable to attend.** No word from you means your host is waiting for you.
- Even if your plans are unusual, it's always courteous to let others know about them. Simply making a phone call would suffice.

What if you just *don't feel like going* on the day of the party?

Unless you're the most popular girl in school/college/office, cancelling at the last minute because you've received a 'better' offer will get your name removed from ALL the invitation lists.

There are only three permissible reasons to rescind a previously given affirmative response:

- serious illness or injury
- a death in the family
- or an unavoidable professional or business conflict

It is imperative that you contact your hosts promptly.

Chapter 11

Let the Good Times Roll

Okay, so you've been invited, you've accepted the invitation, blocked your calendar and decided on your outfit. What are we forgetting?

The Art of Gifting

As a guest, you should know what to gift to the host. A few evergreen options are:

- A cake
- Coffee table books
- Candles

Flowers can sometimes get tricky because the host might feel obliged to place them to make the guest feel like they appreciate the gift, even if it goes against the overall colour palette of the surroundings. Unless you know how the surroundings look, and that the host has no allergy to flowers, it's best to stick with the other options. Think about it, what could go wrong with a candle? Worst case scenario: the host doesn't like the fragrance – they can still place it in the guest bathroom.

What makes a good host or hostess?

- Make sure to welcome each visitor as they arrive. Inform them that you are happy they arrived.
- Give them a welcome drink to help them feel at ease.
- Bring new visitors to existing friends so they can converse while you welcome new ones if there are any.
- Join your friends once everyone who is coming has arrived.
- Spend some time with each group if they tend to break up into smaller groups.
- Make sure everyone is aware of the restroom location.
- Ensure that everyone has everything they need, has eaten and is aware of where to find a beverage.
- A good host also accompanies the guests to the driveway or at least to the door and says goodbye.

Pro tip: When there's a new guest who hasn't met my old friend's group, I inform a close friend of mine (who I think would gel well with the newcomer) to establish a good conversation with them. This puts everyone at ease and the party never gets awkward.

Being a Good Guest

- Say please, thank you and be kind (it looks easy, but more often than not we forget the basics).

- Be friendly and avoid starting fights or confrontations with other visitors.
- Leave the area tidy. Clean up spills at once, and if your wet towel is on the ground, pick it up.
- Offer to help your host or hostess with additional responsibilities, like bringing out meals.
- Enjoy your friend's party and keep in mind that your friend likely put some effort into it; therefore, let your friend know that you value the effort and the invitation.
- Thank your host or hostess, as well as his or her parents, if they are there before you leave.

Notes of Gratitude

Sending thank you notes to the guests who attended your party is essential. Fancy or simple does not matter – just let them know you are delighted they arrived. It is not customary to send party guests expressions of gratitude for their attendance, but doing so would be appreciated.

As a guest, you can call, email, or text your host to express your appreciation for their hospitality and to let them know how much you enjoyed it.

Being a good host or hostess would ensure that people like coming to your parties. Being a good guest will ensure that others continue to invite you.

Always invite guests to your party in advance and give them time to react. Make notes on your invitations about special needs or instructions so they are prepared. If you're organising a beach party and would like your guests to bring their own towels, let them know in the invitation (but also arrange for a few towels to be on the safer side.) Serve alternatives for guests with dietary preferences and make sure the guests are aware.

Chapter 12

Bon Appétit

Preparing the Menu & Asking about Food Allergies

We expect to host friends and family for the holidays and other important occasions so that we may enjoy each other's company while feasting on delicious cuisine and drinking enjoyable beverages. However, we need to consider the dietary restrictions of every person that walks through our door, as the incidence of food allergies and intolerances has skyrocketed in the last decade.

Even if your dinner party attendees have very particular dietary requirements, you can simply meet them. But there are things you can do to make sure everyone who comes to dinner is comfortable and leaves happy.

Below are some ideas for hosting a dinner party where guests with food allergies are welcome.

If you can, try to get information before you go.

You should enquire about any dietary restrictions or allergies that guests may have on the invites. For the sake of safety, you should also inquire as to the degree of their allergy.

Do I have it correct that there will be no invitation cards being sent out? Just ask and jot it down on WhatsApp.

Pro tip: We usually avoid calling this 'dietary restriction' because of the negative connotation attached to the word 'restrict'. The guest may not openly share their allergy thinking it would affect your preparation.

Rally the troops!

- If you are holding a potluck and one or more of your guests has a food allergy, you should ask everyone to bring a dish that does not include the allergen.
- Guests with severe allergies or illnesses like celiac disease can't be accommodated by simply omitting certain ingredients. Be careful not to contaminate anything while preparing or serving food. Realise that a person with celiac disease can't consume even a crumb of bread and that all cooking and serving equipment must be well-cleaned before use.
- Clearly label all foods so that guests know which ones they can partake in.
- While an ordinary handwritten note might work, labels that fit in with the party's colour scheme or aesthetic would be preferable.

- A separate buffet station for guests with special diet requirements should be clearly marked if you have the time and resources to do so (such as those who are gluten-free, dairy-free, vegan, or vegetarian). However, sometimes this can alienate such guests and make them feel uncomfortable. At times, etiquette is best left to the social situation so you should weigh the pros and cons and decide accordingly.

- Leaving a basket of dinner rolls in the middle of the table may seem like a good idea, but it might lead to gluten-free guests ingesting breadcrumbs. If you have at least one gluten-free visitor at your dinner party, it's usually best to avoid gluten altogether. Delicious gluten-free foods are easily available now.

Chapter 13

Raising a Toast!

Take a deep breath, read these guidelines and then stop thinking about how to propose a toast.

Follow the host's lead. It is customary for the event's host to make the opening toast. Like this, "I'm glad you could all join to ring in the New Year with me. Cheers to a fruitful year ahead!"

Bring in the troops. Nothing makes you feel more out of place than standing in front of a group of people, whether they be friends or strangers, and asking them to be quiet while you propose a toast. Instead, raise your glass and ask for the aid of your co-workers and friends by asking them to help calm down their individual groups. An organised lady always has her buddies to help (see, this is why building relationships is important!).

Timing is crucial. A well-prepared and practised toast is guaranteed to be a hit at any event.

Decide the essence of the point you wish to make, and then express it using as few words as possible.

A toast is not a roast.

The shorter the toast, the better. This lets the celebration keep rolling without any interruptions to the flow of discourse.

What if I've already finished my drink?

Oops! If you want to join in on a group toast but realise you're dry, just raise that empty glass (in a pinch) and act like you're about to take a sip.

Forcing everyone to pause their toast while you refill your glass would be rude.

Pro tip: Prepare a glass for a New Year's Eve toast by filling it just before the clock strikes midnight.

Clink or no clink?

- Ignore the urge to smash your drink. Do not signal that you are going to begin your toast by hitting the side of your glass with a butter knife; instead, raise your glass towards the middle of the gathering.
- There's no need to clink glasses. While some believe clinking glasses were supposed to ward off bad spirits, or to show brotherhood, today your sole irate guest may be the host who was unpleasantly surprised to find their pricey champagne flute or wine glass broken.
- Don't be shy about clinking glasses with your companions if the occasion arises, there's no need to go berserk if someone else initiates the ritual.

On our birthdays in school, our teacher would make us stand in front of the class while everyone else sang 'Happy Birthday,' and those were the most awkward two minutes ever.

When we grow up, this turns into such a situation:

Let's say it's your special occasion, maybe you got a promotion – if the host offers a toast in your honour, stop drinking by yourself right now. Keep your drink in your glass until everyone else has finished theirs and their glasses are back on the table. Like clapping oneself on the back, sipping during your own toast would be a sign of self-appreciation.

Always raise a glass to the host. Successfully hosting an event is no easy task, so raising a glass in your host's honour is a great way to express your appreciation.

Use a phrase like, "Thank you, you made a real effort to make tonight memorable, and it shows. Amrita, the wonderful host, deserves a toast."

Chapter 14

Fine Dining

Un-complicating the Complicated

Girls, it's time to make a good impression and brush up on our etiquette skills.

Fine dining can come with nervousness, especially if we don't visit such restaurants often. Chances are you'd have to attend at least one business/social meeting at a fancy restaurant in your life.

While common sense is always the best way to go, using the following tips can make you look more put together in the fine-dine world.

First and foremost, remember you are the guest. Calm down. There's no reason to feel uncomfortable.

While networking, don't do anything that requires both hands to be held. If you must stand, use only one hand to hold a drink or a plate of food. Make sure your hand is dry before extending a solid but not crushing handshake by holding a drink in your left hand.

While sitting is acceptable for consuming beverages, meeting and greeting guests requires standing. Engage in meaningful eye contact.

The Proper Procedure for Entering and Taking a Seat at a Dining Table

- Make sure you don't miss the gathering by being late, and if you are going to be late, give them a call.
- Do not set anything down on the table, including bags, purses, sunglasses, cell phones, and briefcases.
- Keep your elbows off the table and keep an upright stance.
- Ignore your phone for 15 minutes before phoning to see whether your dinner companions are late.

PLACING AN ORDER

- Unless your host specifically tells you to, you shouldn't get the priciest dish on the menu, any extras or dessert. It's better to avoid ordering alcohol, but if the host does, it's fine to drink in moderation.
- Don't get something that's going to be a hassle to consume (i.e., spaghetti, French onion soup). The same applies if you're out on a date (unless you really want to, in which case, you go, girl!).

- Saying 'thank you' to the butler is fine while they serve you for the first and last time, but thanking them every time is not a good practice (unlike what it may seem). In the olden days, butlers were supposed to be the magic genies who would make everything appear on the table while the host and guests enjoyed their meal and conversation. Thanking them too many times implies they're not doing their job correctly, and this can come off as rude, even if that's not your intention.

- Wait until everyone has been served before starting to eat unless the person who has not yet been served gives the okay.

CUTLERY

- If you're given a choice of eating with utensils, start at the outside and work your way in as a rule of thumb. In the case of two forks, for instance, the outer fork should be used first.
- Never make a fist with your utensils or use them as a talking tool. If you must talk, place the cutlery down.

- Don't leave your utensils on the table; instead, place them on your plate.

NAPKIN

- After sitting down at the table, you should place your napkin on your lap (folded in half with the fold towards your waist), but you should always follow your host's lead.
- Keep the napkin on your lap for the duration of the dinner. If you want the waiter to know you'll be back, place your napkin on your chair or to the left of your plate.
- The meal is over when the host puts their napkin down. Then, lay your napkin face up on the table. You need not fold it as neatly as you got it, simply to show that you've used it and it needs to go for cleaning. Etiquette also involves making it easier for the server to know what to do next.

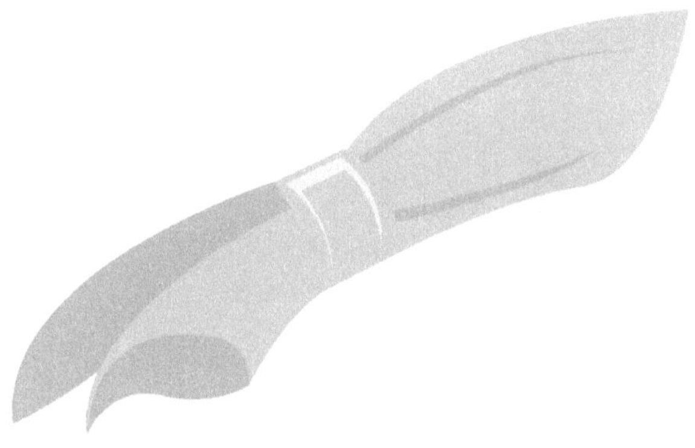

Chapter 15

Customs at the Table

Now that we know the basics, what happens when your food comes to the table?

- Cut your food into little pieces and chew it thoroughly before swallowing. And please, puh-lease, don't chat when you're eating, and chew with your mouth closed.
- To the right, please pass the food (i.e., bread, salad dressings). If you're the one who's supposed to pass the breadbasket around, you should start by giving some to the person to your right, then to the left, and serve yourself last. Using a knife, put a bit of butter on the side of your bread plate. Also, ladies, bread (including croissants) must always be eaten by hand.

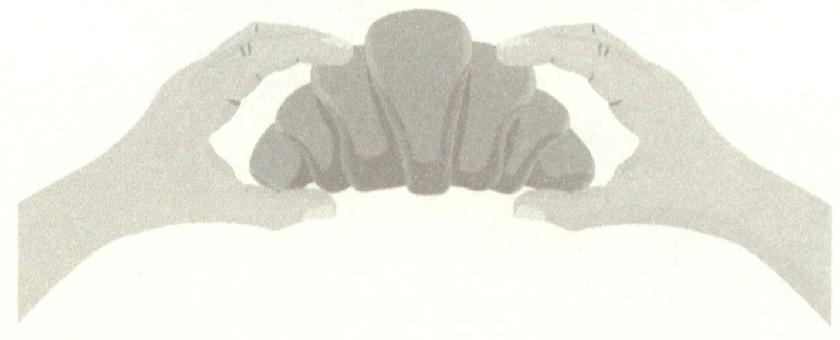

- Do not use a knife to cut the bread, and don't consume it uncut either. Break a bite-sized section with your hands.

- Don't just pass salt or pepper individually; pass them both together. If you have been asked to send these forward, you should not stop to use them.

- Use 'b' and 'd' to remember the placement of bread and drinks on the table. Make lower case letters 'b' (left hand) and 'd' (right hand) with your fingers. Bread (b) goes on the top left, and drinks (d) go on the right of the plate.

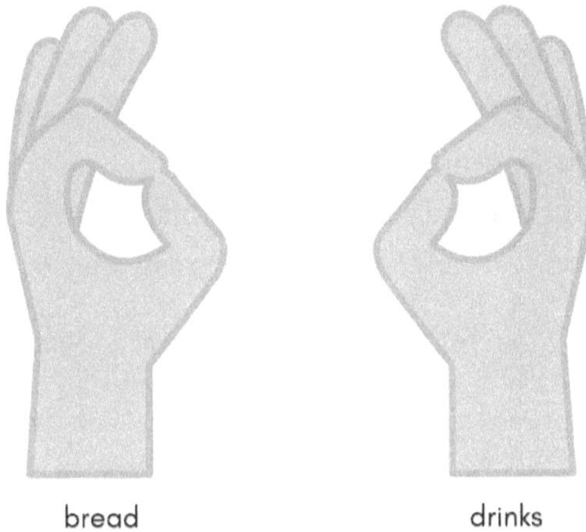

- Keep your cutlery straight to wind up the meal and at an angle, if you're just pausing.

- Instead of blowing on your soup to chill it, try gently stirring it in a crescent shape. Take the soup spoon in the direction that is away from your face, make sure it doesn't drip down and then sip.

When I was a kid, my grandma used to say:

"The soup goes out, then it goes in my mouth."

- It is okay to not finish everything on your plate. Leaving some food/drink on your plate/glass is considered courteous in some cultures since it shows there was plenty. While in other cultures, this can seem as wastage and show the host you didn't like it. Etiquette involves being respectful of the local culture.

Respecting Cultures & Their Meals

- **European or Continental**: Use your left hand to hold the food as you use your right hand to chop it.
- **In South Asian Cultures**: It is common practice to eat rice or roti with your hands.
- **In Asian Cultures**: Chopsticks are used, so if you are going for a

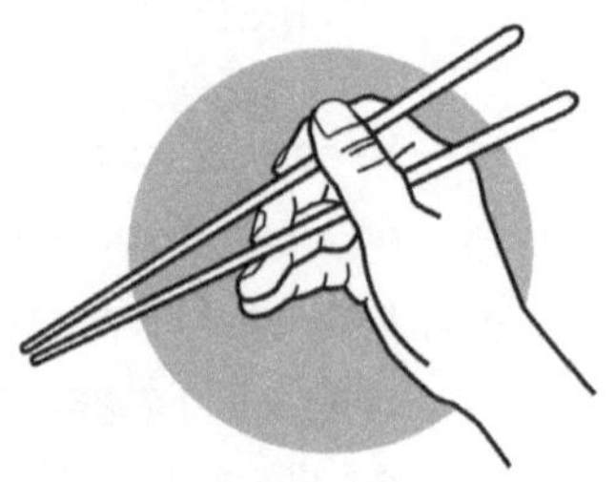

meal at a fine-dine Asian restaurant, it is always good to practice beforehand.

- **In the US**: Cut with your right hand, hold with your left, then swap hands to eat with your right.

After you have completed, leave your dishes where they are and don't stack them when you're done eating.

The host typically foots the bill and leaves a suitable tip (15% for satisfactory service, 20% for outstanding performance) for the wait staff.

The universal 'social survival kit'

- Make sure you have a detailed seating arrangement planned if you are the host. Most diplomatic events worldwide follow the French seating and table arrangement since diplomacy comes from France. Inquire about protocol before attending a formal state dinner.

- It's considered impolite to sit down at a dinner table before the hostess and to get up before she does. Wait until the host begins eating before diving into your meal (even if it's the only thing you've been craving all day).

- While seated, unfold your napkin and place it on your knees (not your neck or collar).

- Before serving the men at the table, begin with the woman to your immediate right. Traditionally, men were supposed to fill women's glasses at all times. If this is okay by you, let the man sitting next to you do it.

- Avoid eating with your hands (especially chicken legs, ugh!), complaining about the meal, drinking the entire glass at once, picking your teeth and licking your cutlery.

- Do not 'gesticulate' with your cutlery in your hands, eat with your mouth wide open, slurp, talk or drink while your mouth is full.

- Avoid using the toilet once everyone has started eating dinner. Wait till the dinner is over (unless you absolutely can't, in which case the graceful thing would be to politely excuse yourself).

- If you need to take a break during your meal, don't just set your cutlery down on the table; instead, place it crossed on your plate or in the knife holder if present.

- Lips should be wiped gently before and after drinking (without leaving bold food or lipstick marks on the napkin).

- It's rude to reach across the table for something like salt or water; instead, politely request that it be passed to you.

- It's essential to remember that the fork tines **always remain pointed down** and the sharp end of the knife inwards, towards you, in Continental style, even when you bring your food to your mouth. This comes from the olden days to show others that you would not hurt them.

- Certain cultures are okay with keeping tines up. Most people are probably using their utensils how they were taught to use them so there's never a 'right' or 'wrong' way. Just do what comes naturally to you and avoid judging others for what they're doing (unless of course, they're having noodles with ketchup…).

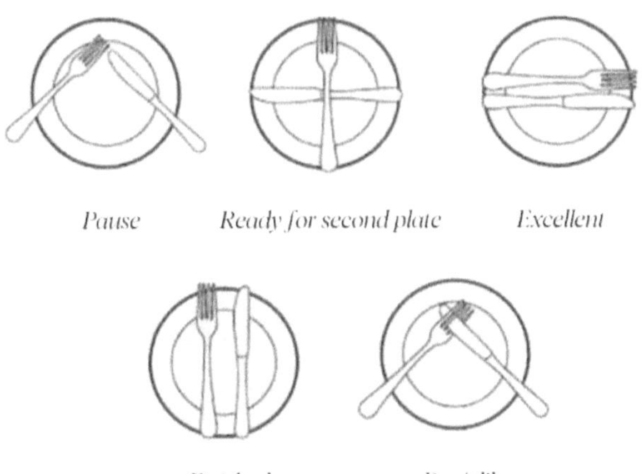

Pause   Ready for second plate   Excellent

Finished   Don't like

Chapter 16

Handling Uncomfortable Questions

Why haven't you had children yet? Why haven't you two gotten married yet? Why did your job end? Why do you remain single?

Truth be told, we all have those nosy relatives who have absolutely no chill. Sometimes they may not even realise they're not supposed to ask these questions. You might be shocked and may even ask yourself, "Really? Did she just say that?"

For all my Princess Diaries fans, imagine what Princess Mia would do in such a situation.

Wit and grace, always.

Strategy #1: Counter Question

The oldest trick in the book is to just avoid the topic with a counter question and a gentle smile. This works for questions that might not be as offensive.

Q: You've gained weight, haven't you? How much do you weigh?

Ans: Why don't you tell me how much you weigh first?

Strategy #2: Clarity

Addressing that you're not comfortable talking about it gives a clear signal to the other person, so they wouldn't ask the question again.

Q: Did you hear about her divorce?

Ans: I'd rather not discuss that.

So, ice cream, strawberry, chocolate or vanilla?

Strategy #3: Laugh It Off

If you're at ease enough, you can just joke around about it without responding to the question.

Q: Being a social media influencer looks so cool! How much do you guys make?

Ans: Haha, it's never enough!

How to Wrap Up an Awkward Conversation?

Nobody is more annoying than the nosy, competitive, self-obsessed cousin you see only at weddings who just

won't. stop. talking.

Even though you stopped to chat for a bit, it's time to leave. Politely exit the conversation by saying:

- We really ought to get together.
- Let's get caught up soon.
- We should go out for a drink or grab a cup of coffee soon.

Pro tip: When you use the word 'should' to suggest that you two should spend more time together, you imply that you two should do so without making any immediate arrangements or commitment to do so.

- A natural winding-up question is, "You have my number, right?" or suggest an alternate means of getting in touch, but do so only if you really want them to text.

Chapter 17

Expressing Condolences

Try as you might, finding the proper words to express your sorrow can be difficult. Unfortunately, difficulties and losses are inevitable. What really counts is how much sympathy you offer to others who are going through tough times. To let the grieving know that you care is the best you can do when comfort is impossible after a death. Be as thoughtful, sincere, kind and polite as possible in your response.

- As soon as you receive credible information, it is proper to make immediate contact with the individual or persons who may be affected.

To communicate effectively, use empathy, consideration and good judgement. It's kind to give someone a call, but if you get voice mail, don't take it personally. It's possible that they are currently inundated with calls and unable to answer each one individually.

- Only visit a grieving family if you are certain your presence will be welcome. Grief and difficulties are something that some individuals would rather deal with alone.
- When attending a funeral or wake, it is proper to spend as much time as possible with the family who has lost

a loved one. The proper way to express sorrow is to soothe the bereaved and offer any help we can. And allowing lots of privacy so they may be as alone or social as they choose.

If you find it easier to express your condolences on paper than in person, you might choose to send a letter, email or text message. However, only use these channels if you are extremely familiar with the deceased and know she is at ease with receiving sympathy notes in this manner.

It's possible that the most impacted person has made a public statement about it on social media. If you contact someone through email, text or social media, it is polite to send a card or letter as a follow-up. When someone you care about is going through a tough time, they will appreciate very much a handwritten card or letter that you took the time to send. Trust me on this.

How to Write Letters of Condolence

What you write will change depending on whether the receiver is a close friend, family member, co-worker, or casual acquaintance.

We'll go through certain ground rules that you should follow.

- Avoid complicated sentences.
- The proper phrases to use while expressing deep sadness include the word 'sorry,' like, "Sorry to hear about your dad."
- Kindness includes sharing an authentic, heartfelt recollection of fondness for the departed.
- When you can, it's nice to offer some kind of useful aid.

*Pro tip: I personally feel **white** is the most common type of sympathy flower colour as it signifies remembrance.*

Also, keep in mind that condolence notes and letters are too individual to be standardised. You should always try to express your sympathies in the way that feels the most natural and genuine to you. Keep in mind that 'less is more' as a rule of thumb.

Chapter 18

Common Sense? Not so Common

Misconduct That Must Never Be Ignored

Here's what an elegant lady would never do:

- **Speaking in the Middle of a Conversation**

When someone is talking, never interrupt them. You may do this subconsciously for attention, out of boredom, or impatience, but please do not. Such a famous pet peeve!

- **Disregarding 'Sorry' & 'Thank You'**

Thank you, sorry and excuse me should always be said when needed. In London, I noticed people thanking the bus driver while getting off. And it wasn't  just a bland 'thank you,' it was a very cheerful, grateful *"Thank you, Driver!"* that brought a smile to my face every time I heard it. It doesn't cost anything to be polite.

- **Responding Arrogantly**

We usually end up picking this habit seeing others around us do the same. Be mindful of your tone and never use the *"Do you know who my dad is?"* card on anyone. It's so not elegant.

- **Cussing and Swearing**

Most of the time, when we use harsh language, it is because we have developed a habit or are frustrated. Take it slow and work on bettering yourself.

- **Ignoring Visitors**

Greet visitors with a "Namaste, uncle or aunty" and then bid them farewell when they leave. Unless you're single-handedly dealing with your company's PR crisis, there's no reason to isolate in your room when you have guests over.

Chapter 19

*Break That Glass Ceiling
(But Also Account for Fixing it)*

Stipend / Salary Negotiations

If you're just starting out in your career, one of the best ways to negotiate a higher compensation is to respectfully point to a specific reason that shows why your performance deserves a higher salary.

"It was wonderful news to receive your letter of employment offer. I'm interested in the position, but I was hoping for an extra 20% because I've been able to enhance team productivity by 30% through automation in each of my three data science internships."

The pay-negotiating process can involve back-and-forth dialogue, so don't let the stress of starting a negotiation distract you from your goal. Salary negotiations are an opportunity to make a positive first impression; therefore, it's crucial to act professionally and courteously at all times.

84

There are three possible responses an employer can have to your salary-negotiation strategies:

- They may accept counteroffers, which means you may have effectively bargained with them.
- They may refuse.
- Or the middle ground: they may counter with a new offer that's higher than their original figure but still short of what you were hoping to earn.

If you plan on negotiating, know your bargaining power.

You can inquire about the salary range for the role by asking the interviewer. As a bonus, it can give you a leg up in starting pay negotiations with confidence.

Don't lock yourself into a poor wage.

Avoid accepting a low range until you have had the chance to negotiate. Keep room for salary negotiation if you get to that point in the interview process.

Introduce yourself and your qualifications.

It is important to prove your worth to potential employers throughout any salary negotiation, especially during an entry-level discussion. It is more important to do this modestly.

If you're interviewing for the position of social media coordinator, you can highlight your value by discussing a successful social media campaign you oversaw while interning. You are welcome to elaborate on the part you played in the campaign, the tactics you employed and the outcomes you saw.

Consider alternate methods of payment (my fav!)

If an employer is unwilling to pay you more because you lack specific abilities, you may be able to negotiate education reimbursement while you earn those certificates. Taking this step can prove to your potential employer that you are dedicated to developing your professional skills.

If you are interviewing for a position that requires a long commute, you may be eligible for transport reimbursement.

An alternative strategy for dealing with a lengthy commute is to inquire about the potential of working remotely at least part of the time. As a result, this can be used as a trade-off for a lower salary without increasing the overall cost to the company.

Pro tip: Out of personal experience, it's important to negotiate your vacation time and benefits without sounding like all you want is to party in Bali. There are many who, given the choice, would take lower pay in exchange for greater me-time. "Yes Sarah, I'm out of the office. I'd like to read five books in 7 days. Goodbye."

If they refuse to pay a higher salary, the company might be having a hard cap on how much it may pay a new hire.

Whether or not you accept the job offer depends on several factors, including the availability of similar positions in the market. When declining a job offer due to pay concerns, do so graciously to show your appreciation for the opportunity.

> *"For this reason, I've resolved to keep looking for work until I discover something that offers a pay more in line with my expectations. The interview for the position at your organisation is really appreciated and I hope to stay in touch."*

Chapter 20

Managing Finances

Have you read that quote, "It is better to cry in a Mercedes than on a scooter?"

My Nani was a teacher, and she used to tell me when she just got married, there was a huge issue about her wanting to have a separate bank account. Not surprisingly, the majority of working women in India do not make their own financial decisions simply because of how we've been conditioned.

While we talk of etiquette, chivalry and dress codes, it is also important in today's day and age; every young lady should try to be financially independent.

Personal money management is a pastime for some and a scary task for others. Regardless, getting out of debt and reaching your financial aims requires careful personal financial planning. Sounds boring (and awfully overwhelming), doesn't it?

Let's clear the clutter:

Decide your most important financial objectives

This will help you see the big picture as you move forward and give you a sense of where you're headed financially. Will you be taking your family on a vacation next summer, and if so, how much money do you need to save? Is it your intention to begin saving ten percent of your salary to secure your financial future in old age?

Pro tip: Don't stress if setting a far-reaching objective seems too daunting. On the contrary, focus on the not-too-distant future. By dividing massive aims into manageable portions (and lesser sums of money), they become much more manageable.

Prepping for it

With these targets in mind, you'll be more likely to stick to a spending plan, set up savings auto-pay, and avoid taking on any new debt. After that, you'll be in a better position to start making long-term financial goals, like saving for retirement, building an emergency fund and investing.

Finding possible roadblocks and developing strategies for overcoming them

This is important so you can avoid falling flat on your face *(and thus, avoid spending on another bottle of your favourite foundation)* when life throws a wrench in your plans by making a backup plan before anything goes wrong.

Making it part of your routine

The amount of money you have available to spend every month is decided by your budget, which you create. Take out your glitter

pens and coloured papers
(yes, the ones you've been
saving for a special day)
and break this down.

**Keep tabs on your
spending**

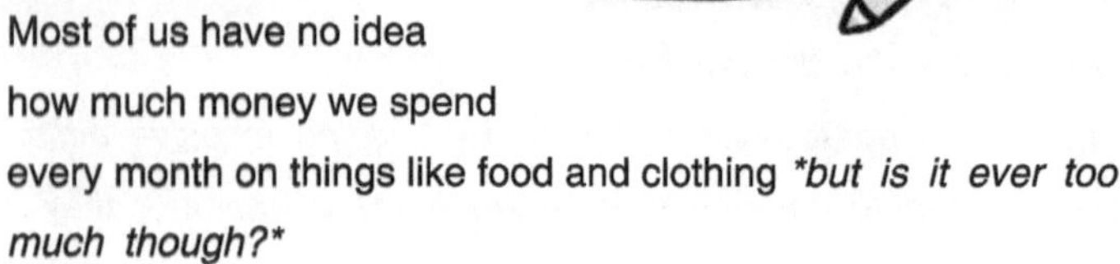

Most of us have no idea
how much money we spend
every month on things like food and clothing *but is it ever too
much though?*

Keeping tabs on your expenditures might prove to be an
enlightening exercise, one that causes you to breathe in and
breathe out. You might end up finding that you spend more than
Rs. 5000 a month on online food orders. Now I love a good
biryani at my doorstep, but can we cook that biryani at times and
save up? Yes, of course.

Stay debt-free

This should be a priority. Managing your debt and cutting it will
offer you a sense of accomplishment, and accomplishment itself
may be a stress reliever as you make progress towards your goal
of financial freedom.

Set up auto-payments

People who master personal finance never miss a payment
and prioritise their own financial needs. Every month, they do
this without any conscious effort since they have these tasks
automated. Set up your rent/phone bill payment / any other

regular bills, so that you always pay the amount due. Doing so will also safeguard your credit rating.

Unobvious (but creative) tools

Credit card reward points for free vacations, cash back on petrol and groceries, and other money-saving techniques are common among those who have mastered personal finance.

Tally up all the loyalty points, gift cards, and other vouchers you have accumulated for things like hotel stays, coffee and even a night at the movies.

Chapter 21

How to Walk Right

Princesses in training, it's time to carry yourselves with pride.

Before I went on stage during my graduation ceremony, I was terrified (I blame stage fright!). So what did I do?

Stretched out in private and took note of the expansion of space as I straightened my back and shoulders. There you go, the secret boost of confidence.

- Extend your spine as if you were being lifted by the top of your head. Maintain a flat back and a firm core; don't arch your back or tuck your tailbone.
- The strain on your upper back and neck increases if you keep your gaze on the ground. Look in front of you, somewhere between 10 and 20 feet.
- Shoulders rolled back and down, tension released. Rather than being dragged up towards the ears, your shoulders should be in a relaxed position while you walk. This also makes room for a more natural arm swing.
- Don't restrict your motion by locking your elbows. Move your arms in a pendulum motion, forward and back gently. Please don't let them go above your chest or

across your body *(unless you want to be in the next Happy Feet movie).*

- Instead of landing flat-footed with a thud, you should be rolling from heel to toe as you stride.
- While walking down a flight of stairs, avoid looking downwards. Gently put your fingers on the railing and glide downwards with a straight, elegant posture.

Pro tip: There's nothing more regretful than uncomfortable footwear. I had been eyeing a pair of heels from my favourite designer. When I went to buy them, they just had one size available which was half a size smaller than mine. I convinced myself to buy it, but clearly, I wasn't Cinderella. Go for a shoe size that allows your foot to breathe instead of feeling like it has been jailed. If you aren't used to wearing heels, try buying heel pads and insoles.

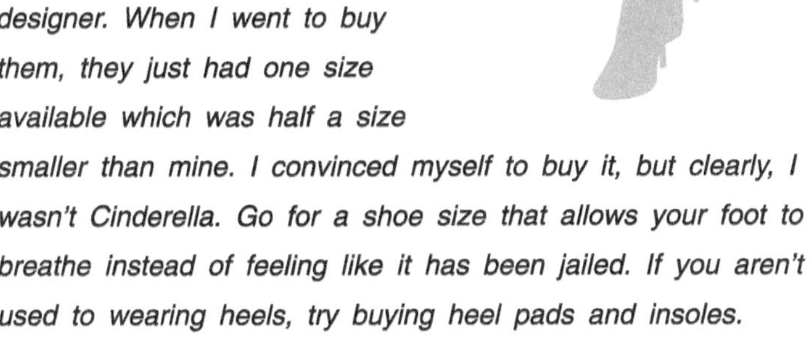

Wear your new shoes on a variety of surfaces around the house for at least 30 to 45 minutes. This will provide you with a decent notion of how well your shoes support your feet. If you only wear them inside, you won't have sullied their purity yet, so you have the option to return or swap them.

Don't assume that a pair of shoes will extend a little after a few wears; this isn't always the case.

It's crucial to choose the appropriate shoes, but it's also crucial to treat them right. Check the forecast before leaving the house to prevent an embarrassing shoe emergency. If it's raining, you risk ruining your leather boots, and if it's freezing, you could hurt yourself if you wear high heels.

Let's say you're simply sipping your wine and minding your business, stand bringing one foot slightly forward and turning the back foot to a 45-degree angle. Bring the back of the heel of your front foot close to the instep of the back foot and once you have the weight on one leg, you are free to move the other leg slightly as soon as someone comes to meet you.

Effortless grace really takes a lot of effort in order to look effortless.

Chapter 22

Sitting Elegantly is an Art

Etiquette means behaving a little better than is absolutely essential.

Will Cuppy

When we learn how to use subtle cues in our communication – from posture and expressions to word choice and tone of voice – we can make a positive impression and advance our personal and professional life.

Let's get our imagination hats on: imagine a helium balloon gently pulling your head up, a rat running behind your back on the chair (so keep it straight or it can touch you), and a cat on your lap (you don't want it to bump your belly against it, so sit upright).

The most charming and polite manner to sit in with the feet crossed at the ankles. Your knees and toes should be in a straight line. Put your legs in a slightly angled position.

Put people at rest by not appearing overly uptight and by keeping your hands on your thighs.

Tadaa – this is how you can royalty sit. You're ready, princess! All that is required now is some patience and practice.

Remember that these are simply guidelines. Many prefer sitting cross-legged when the situation is appropriate. What you read here is for the highest level of formal appearances, so pick and choose what you'd like to practice daily.

- **Do not block yourself**

When a woman blocks her purse in front of her body, she is restricting her own access to her purse. Politicians and actors who wish to appear less approachable in public instinctively shield their bodies with their pocketbooks.

- **Point your feet**

A person's attitude can be seen in their feet. Feet that are pointing directly at another person show that person has the individual's full attention. But if they're facing away from you or out the door, it could be a sign that they'd rather be somewhere else.

- **Don't minimise your appearance**

When women are anxious, they often try to minimise their physical presence by crossing their knees, tucking their arms into the chair or folding them over their chest. If you're feeling tense or nervous, relieve some of that tension by putting your feet flat

on the ground and squeezing your toes
together (nobody will know but you).

- **Play to your strengths**

Conversing with someone
on your dominant side
(whether right or left) can
boost your self-esteem while
conversing on your non-
dominant side can make you
feel unsure of yourself.

Chapter 23

Decoding Dress Codes (& Why They Exist)

Turning dress codes from a nightmare into a pleasant fantasy

Have you ever found yourself at a loss for what to wear when you receive an invitation? Even when a lady goes clubbing, good clubs ask guests to follow a certain kind of dressing, and they do this simply to maintain the aura of the place.

calls bestie to ask what she's wearing

Confused? To be honest, no one is surprised. It can feel like a nightmare trying to figure out the difference between dressy casual, smart casual, black tie and black tie optional.

Casual / Informal / Come as You are

With a relaxed dress policy, feel free to wear whatever makes you feel good. This dress code is flexible enough to accommodate both skirts and heels and shorts and T-shirts. You can't go wrong with whatever you wear, but just no sweats or PJs.

Casual Chic

Wearing your most gorgeous weekend outfit is encouraged when the dress code is 'dressy casual'. Your sense of style will be put to the test by this dress code, which is only a notch above your most laidback getup. Pick out a skirt and a short-sleeved button-up shirt and accessorise with everything from a necklace and a scarf to a pair of platform sandals. Make sure to keep a refined air, though. In a hurry? An alternative winning style is nice jeans teamed with heels.

Semi-Formal

This is a grade below black tie, but still a notch over cocktail clothing. One of the simplest and most effective ways to succeed at this dress code is to wear a little black dress. Find a dress that stops at, or just above, the knee (make sure the hemline is at least two inches above your knee).

Formal / Black Tie / Black Tie Optional

This dress code isn't as complicated as it may seem. Black tie optional just means that guests can choose to wear their most formal outfit, such as an evening gown, but they also have the choice to wear a cocktail dress.

What should you not wear to a black tie optional event? Anything casual, including flats, sneakers, pastel colours, breezy sundresses, crop tops and so on.

To give you some context into how seriously dress codes are to be taken, when I was filming with the Prince of Mewar in Udaipur, their staff specifically briefed us on what to wear before the shoot.

Pro tip: If you're helping the men in your life dress up, remember, they have to wear a tie. Even though the invite might say a black tie is 'optional,' a dark, subdued colour tie is indispensable, whether that be a necktie or a bow tie. While the majority of black tie optional events take place in the evening, light-coloured suits are ideal for daytime occasions.

White Tie

The original formal dress code, white tie, is thought to be the pinnacle of elegance. A full-length evening gown for women is expected (a short dress won't be warmly received).

Chapter 24

Wardrobe Essentials Every Lady Must Have

Have you at some point stood in front of your wardrobe, staring at the clothes hanging inside (or the pile of clothes on the floor of your bedroom)? I probably shouldn't even be asking… it's okay, we all do it.

It's not that you have nothing to wear; rather, you're either at a loss as to what to dress because you lack a cohesive wardrobe or you're at a loss because you lack a cohesive wardrobe.

Whoops, let's fix it.

The biggest pro tip of all: Choosing pieces that complement one another when you shop is the secret to a versatile closet. Any closet can receive help from a foundation of neutral fundamentals.

Here are the six items that are important for any lady's closet:

- **A (well-fitted) plain white tee.** This wardrobe staple looks great with pants, shorts, skirts and basically everything. It's as versatile as it gets. Dress it up with a jacket and accessories, or go for a more laidback look with some shorts and sneakers. Make sure you get a high-quality basic T-shirt even if that means it's slightly more expensive, simply because it'll last you for years compared to a cheaper one that might lose its appeal in just a few washes.

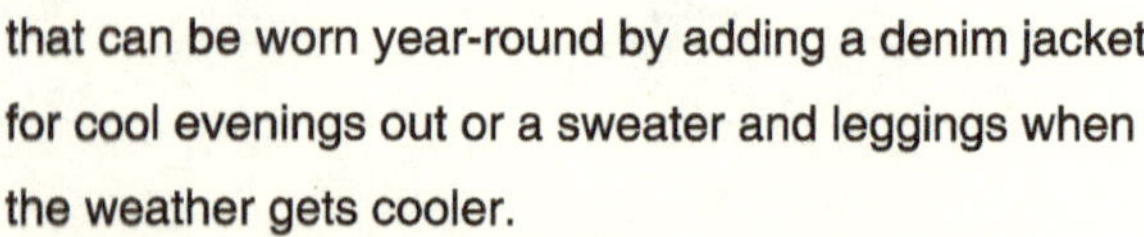

- **A summer dress.** Find one that can be worn year-round by adding a denim jacket for cool evenings out or a sweater and leggings when the weather gets cooler.
- **A Denim Jacket.** As fashionable as it is practical, serving as an ideal outer layer in the autumn and

spring, this is also a standalone stunner in the colder months.

- **A Pullover.** Combinable with denim. Combinable with skirts. Throw it on top of a dress. Put on some tights. Put it on your hips. Put it on as your nightwear. If you don't believe me, just ask any teenager. It's crucial to have.

- **Leggings and Jeans.** There are typically two types of ladies: jean lovers and jean haters (aka legging-lovers). Some people adore both, but most people have strong feelings for only one. In terms of timeless appeal, a pair of straight-leg jeans is unrivalled, and in terms of wearability, leggings are unparalleled.

- **Undergarments.** Ideally, a lady would have at least seven to ten sets of underwear. Invest in some new underwear if the old ones are causing discomfort. Nothing restricting or baggy should be worn. The clothes you wear become an extension of your own body. You should feel safe and assured in their care. When worn even once, underwear, socks, undershirts, intimates, pants, bras, lingerie, busters and stockings must be washed. Do not flip it inside-out and wear it again, please (Trust me, I've heard people do this.

Super gross). This is a no-brainer from a health and sanitation perspective and should be adhered to without question.

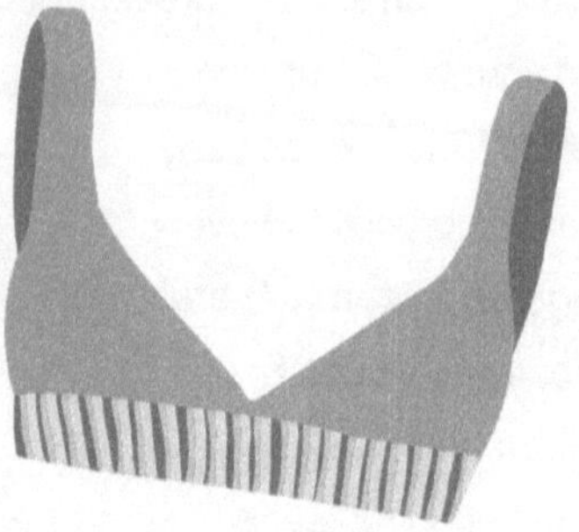

Chapter 25

Your Shopping Guide

Fun as it is to shop, it can be easy to let your attention wander. There are so many places and products to choose from, it's easy to become side-tracked and end up buying something we didn't intend to.

Do yourself a favour and shop wisely to simplify your life. Keep this shopping checklist in mind so that your next trip to the mall is stress-free and you leave the store with everything you came for rather than a bunch of trinkets you won't ever use.

- **Take a list with you**. Instead of trying to remember what you forgot at the billing counter, you can just cross off each item as you travel home. If you don't know your way through all of the aisles, it's best to just ask.
- **Keeping a record of your recent purchases** is an excellent method to keep tabs on how much money you're spending each month on retail therapy.
- **Know what you have** in your closet so you may avoid buying duplicates.

- **Purging your closet of items you no longer wear** should rank among your first priorities. You could donate or re-sell those clothes.

- It's wise to buy **fewer but newer** and more expensive items, especially when it comes to basics like shirts and dresses.

- Get a **loyalty membership** or follow the brand's Instagram handle to stay updated on all the newest bargains and sales.

- When making an online purchase, it's always a good idea to **check for the same item on other sites** so you can compare prices and see the item from different angles.

- *Pro tip: If you're looking for a long-lasting outfit, white probably isn't it because it won't stay white after a couple of washes (and wine spills – been there, done that).*

- Avoid being stuck in a huge line outside of a clothes store's try-on area. It's not worth it to waste so much time. If the line to the dressing rooms is too long to bear, check the return/exchange policy and **try the garment at home.**

- If you're trying the outfit in-store, **consider bringing along two sizes** that you're between just in case one doesn't work out. You won't have to wait in line again only to try on a lower size of the jeans you originally chose.

- When trying on new clothes, **try moving around a bit**. Try sitting, bending, and walking around to feel for pinching, ripping, or any other problems.

- If you're on the fence about buying the outfit, it's best to **wait until you get home to make up your mind**. It would hurt more to throw away a fresh new dress than to go shopping twice in one day.

If there's anything 'Confessions of a Shopaholic' taught us, it is to go after the damn green scarf. If your ideal dress goes on sale, buy it even if you don't think you'll be able to use it right away. A lady knows where to draw the link between wasteful expenditure and treating herself.

Chapter 26

The Art of Letting Go

Look, I get it, friendships (and relationships, in general) can sometimes be draining, especially if you're the one investing time, energy and effort into it more than your friend.

There are three main reasons for such bonds to end:

- the friendship fades gently and organically (the natural fade).
- the friendship becomes toxic.
- the connection no longer delivers value for both parties.

If you're having doubts about a friendship, it's important to pay attention to how you feel around the person and when you're not with them. If you want to learn more about something or analyse it, all you must do is observe it.

Natural Decay of Relationship

After our school farewell, even though my friends and I promised to stay in touch, distance developed and communication broke down. We all progress in our own lives. That's how most people's lives go, and it's how we all learn and develop. You might try asking yourself things like, "Are we entering a new era of life (such as graduating college or moving)?"

Harmful Friendships

In the case of a toxic friendship, it may be best to end communication, move on and devote your time and energy to individuals who add value to your life. This condition arises when a person treats you badly and the connection between you two causes you distress. Questions to ask yourself include: "How do I feel after spending time with this person?"

Destiny's Finale

The third scenario is when you've come to terms with the fact that some facets of your friendship no longer serve you and you'd like to go on without them playing a major role in your life.

Take the case where this friend of yours seems to only have a good time when you're out drinking. Despite initiating time together in other activities that feed your soul and develop your relationship, they don't put in the effort. Or perhaps there's a touch of selfishness that, although not malevolent, leaves you wanting more from the partnership.

Find out if you disagree on topics of importance to you both and whether or not this indicates a serious rift in your views. While we should take care not to be overly critical or to set unreasonable expectations, you may have reached the necessary end if there are aspects of the friendship that are causing you genuine distress.

This is the most difficult of the three since it calls for an actual discussion to be had with the friend.

It's not always pleasant, but it's essential.

There are definite principles of politeness to bear in mind, but what you really say is up to your discretion based on the duration and depth of the friendship.

Do not engage in the conversation by text. This shows a lack of respect for the other person and a lack of maturity and courage on your part. Talk on call or meet face-to-face.

Do not try to trick the other person into thinking you still care by saying something like, "I'm extremely busy now, can I call later?" if you intend to permanently cut relations. Instead, say "I've been giving our friendship some thought, and while I've loved our time together, I've recognised that we have different... [fill in the blank] and I think it would be better if we went our own ways."

Changing your perspective isn't easy, but life is always evolving. In the long run, you'll do yourself and the people around you a favour if you give some thought to the friendships you maintain, keep those that support your mental health and always treat them with compassion.

Remember, stick with people who pull the magic out of you, not the madness.

Chapter 27

The Dating Game

Let's Find Prince Charming!

It's a match! You're going on a date! Good dating etiquette is all about making the other person feel at ease and setting up a positive impression.

It's no secret that there's an unspoken set of rules that govern the dating scene, just as there are for any other game.

- **Stay on time.** The date is off to a bad start if you arrive thirty minutes late without calling to apologise. Never keep your date waiting. Inform your date in advance if you expect to be late. Okay, but what if their phone isn't reachable? Call the venue and ask them to inform your date.

- Regardless of how bad of a day you've had, try to **maintain a pleasant demeanour** for your date. This guideline applies equally well

to a first date as it does to an 81ˢᵗ. Dates shouldn't be awkward or boring. On a date, it's also important to have a pleasant demeanour with the staff. If you get angry with the waiter, you will ruin your, your date's and the waiter's mood.

- **Avoid going 'all hands' on your darling** until you've established some sort of commitment to each other, at least if you're looking for something serious. This is a certain method of making someone very uneasy, very quickly. It's also considered impolite to inquire about a date's physical history during the courtship phase.

Sana's Movie recommendation:

'He's Just Not That Into You'

Who Should Pay the Bill?

Ah, the awkwardness!

Although it was once customary for the male to foot the bill on a date, the norm today is that whoever sets up the date should pay for it. This is true regardless of your gender.

Similarly, if you (a lady) arrange an official dinner with your client (a man), you are the host and your client, the guest. So you'd be taking the cheque once the server presents it.

Be mindful when you make reservations at restaurants. Good restaurants take note of the name under which the reservation is made (considering they are the host) and hand over the bill to that person.

Think about how you look when you get dressed. Don't go and spend all your money on a Gucci outfit just because. All you need to do is display that you care about your looks and their time by dressing correctly for the occasion. You owe it to your date to dress nicely, smell great and have your hair groomed.

If you take your date out, stay with them the whole time. A date has to feel like they are a priority for you. Decide the venue or activity you'll be doing considering mutual interests.

Don't try to impersonate someone else, just be who you really are and put your best foot forward. If there's no chemistry between you and your date, it's important to be open and tell them so in a kind way.

After the Date

Casually let them know how much fun you had with a text message. If you want to go out with that person again, this is the greatest approach. Not everything needs to be a long, flowery letter about how wonderful your experience was.

The traditional three-day courtship period is now considered archaic and unnecessary. The text can be sent the same day or the day after your date.

"Yesterday, I really enjoyed our time together and I hope we get to do it again soon!"

Or

"I had a wonderful time the other day. Let's get coffee next Tuesday if that works for you?"

Pro tip: While my grandma says a lady never asks a man out on a date, times have changed and it's absolutely perfect to ask him out. What's not okay is to pester him if he doesn't seem interested.

hello!
ONLINE DATING
ONLINE DATING

Chapter 28

A Lady in the Cyberspace

Cyber etiquette refers to the rules of conduct that netizens follow to have productive conversations with one another.

- A tech-savvy lady should use professional-looking typefaces in her email responses, answer quickly to messages, avoid rambling and not become unduly emotional in conversations.

- Uppercase = yelling: Do not use all capital letters when chatting or emailing. If you wish to stress a certain word, simply highlight it.

- Just like you would in the real world, it's best to avoid using the Internet for gossip.

- Online social networks such as Instagram, Facebook and Reddit, are user-friendly but that doesn't imply they're fool-proof. Hackers earn their bread and butter doing this. This is

where strong passwords, privacy settings, two-factor authentication and digital literacy help.

- **Never act on impulse**. It may be tempting to express your feelings to others but refrain from saying anything that might be taken the wrong way.

- It's easy to gain followers by often posting images that are revealing. It's one thing to post a bikini photo from your latest trip to the beach, and it's another to post a photo twerking.

- **Avoid showing off**. Great that you got yourself a new phone or a designer bag. Nothing good comes out of bragging online. In fact, most people do this for validation, and an elegant lady has enough confidence already.

Before I hit 'post' on any photo on my IG, I imagine my grandma. Imagine yours or another person who you genuinely like and whose lifestyle you admire.

Would what you're posting make them happy? If she knew you were saying or writing that tweet, would she feel a bit embarrassed? If the response is that grandma wouldn't approve, you will probably regret doing it.

- Don't feel obligated to use every social media app either. Social media is not who you are. Your worth as a person does not depend on how many followers you have. Some of my favourite people have no social media presence at all.

Pro tip: Pinterest may occasionally be a great source of inspiration for bettering aspects of your life, perhaps you need some inspiration for remodelling your wardrobe or a room.

It's easy to want to be perfect like everyone in those pictures. However, when you search for 'brown balayage hair,' you only see perfectly styled hair, nothing else about the person. Do you see how this could be an issue?

Someone might have the perfect Pinterest-worthy wardrobe, but then their house is a mess (and that's what we don't see). Social media has a way of making everything look perfect.

Just keep in mind that perfection is a myth.

Chapter 29

Keeping it Minimal

Minimalism is a lifestyle choice that prioritises simplicity, functionality and mindfulness. It is becoming increasingly popular as people look to simplify their lives and reduce clutter and distractions, and believe me, it helps.

Here are some steps to get started:

- **De-clutter your space:** Start with a room-by-room analysis of your belongings and get rid of anything that doesn't serve a purpose or bring you joy. This activity always gets one's feminine energy up and running.
- **Simplify your life:** Minimalism is not just about reducing physical clutter but also reducing mental clutter. Prioritise your responsibilities and focus on what is essential.
- **Embrace mindfulness:** Minimalism involves being mindful of your thoughts, habits and relationships. Focus on what is truly meaningful to you and let go of what is not.

- **Be intentional with your purchases**: Before making a purchase, ask yourself if it aligns with your values and if it is necessary.
- **Practice gratitude**: A lady who is truly grateful takes time to appreciate what she has and focus on the positive aspects of life.

By embracing minimalism and simplifying your life, you can create more space and time for what is enormously important to you. This can lead to increased happiness, peace of mind and a greater sense of purpose. You also won't need any Vitamin C serums because, with stress out of the way, you'll be glowing from within!

Chapter 30

Organising Your Life

I absolutely love lists of everything. They are specific and focused, and you can put into perspective a lot of important data in a relatively short amount of time.

They also serve as an amazing way to organise, and getting organised is one of the essential ingredients in the recipe for ~ balance ~

Simply put, organising your life is therapeutic. Making disordered chaos clean, tidy and orderly is very satisfying. Plus, when everything is organised, you feel less anxious.

5 ways to get seriously organised

- **Write it down.** If you are keeping your tasks and information in your head, you cannot systematise them. Or perhaps you can, but it will be very difficult. Write down anything that comes to mind, then put it all into lists, calendars and checklists. I like to have my week organised early on, of course leaving some room for last-minute plans. Make sure to prioritise the most important tasks. Take time to reflect on what is enormously important to you, both in the short term and long term. Make a list of your goals and values. Break down your long-term goals into smaller, achievable tasks.

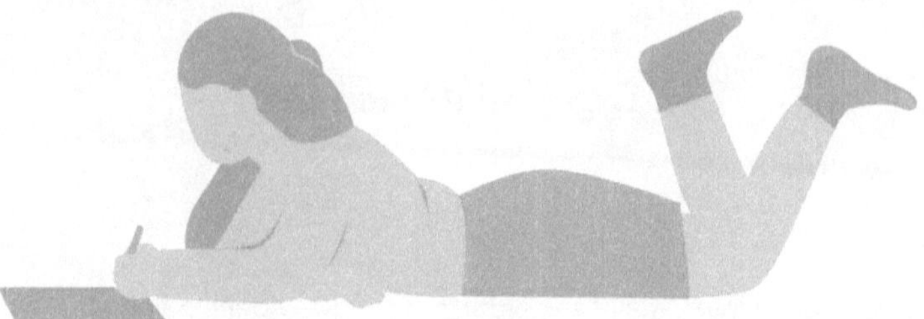

Pro tip: I've created a digital planner on my phone's notes app; it has the date and day followed by my to-do list. You can make emojis and decorate the note as well! Keeping it digital helps me quickly delete work that's done. My mum used to love her physical diary to maintain her to-do list. See what works for you and make it part of your everyday routine.

- **Digital de-clutter.** If you frequently work on a computer/smartphone/tablet, this is very crucial. It's really simple to pile up files on your devices to the point where you find yourself taking five times longer than necessary to do a straightforward activity. Organise your folders, clear your phone's photos (yes, delete photos you'll never see again or put them into folders on a hard drive), delete unused accounts on websites in a single sitting, saving yourself from having to delete hundreds of pointless spam mails in the future.
- **De-clutter your surroundings.** Your life will feel much more organised if your house is in order; so. if you

can, put dividers in every drawer, put on matching bedsheets and pillow covers, and keep your handbags neat and tidy (and take out all the bills you stuff in it the same night).

- **Throw away any expired products.** This is called 'invisible clutter.' The most we can do is dispose of them and learn a lesson (i.e., to plan your purchases). Cosmetics once used are unfit for donation.

- **Keep a calendar of birthdays.** This is something you truly want if you're often forgetting birthdays and anniversaries. Maintaining your relationships is important, and people value you much more if you remember what they've told you. If your friend briefly mentioned their dad's birthday, put it on your calendar or any other app that helps (there are a lot of them). We're all busy, but a simple wish will show respect and genuine care.

This may seem like a lot of work, but you can always make things simpler by starting small and planning ahead. I promise, one of the best things you can do for your family, job and yourself is to organise your life. If you're still on the fence about it, just go for it!

Chapter 31

Seriously Slowing Down

Ever felt like shouting ARGHHHH! when your boss sends you a 'quick task' just as you're about to leave office? And then when you reach home, your brother ends up arguing with you over who ate the ice cream. Life is difficult.

Slowing down just means taking time to reflect and recharge. In today's fast-paced world, it's easy to become caught up in the hustle and bustle of everyday life, but taking the time to slow down is almost essential for your well-being.

Take a step back, breathe and appreciate life as it comes. It's not about becoming a sloth and lounging on the couch all day (although a lazy Sunday is always nice). It's about finding a way to live life in a more mindful and intentional way.

Nature

Spend some time outdoors, whether it's a walk in the park or simply sitting on your porch and enjoying the scenery. The great outdoors has a way of putting things into perspective.

Mindfulness

Focus on the present moment and let go of worries about the future or regrets about the past. Take deep breaths, stretch, and clear your mind.

Laughter

Don't take life too seriously and find time to enjoy the little things. Whether it's a funny meme, a TV show, or a good book, laughter can help you relax and recharge.

Me-time

Set aside time each day to do something you love, whether it's reading a book, taking a bath or just sitting quietly.

Therapy

It helps more than we think it does. I used to think what can a therapist possibly say that I already wouldn't know, and while there's honestly no clear answer I have for that even today, what I do know after taking therapy for over two years is that it changed my life. It has made me more stable, it helped me understand myself and how my mind works, and thus, be there for myself and others in the best way I can.

I wish the whole world could take therapy, it'd be such a nice place.

Remember, life is meant to be enjoyed, not endured. Take a deep breath, slow down, laugh off the bad days and remember, the sun will rise again, and we will try again.

Chapter 32

Be Selfish with Self-Care

To put it bluntly, life doesn't always go according to plan. Your emotional health may suffer when you encounter difficulties (even princesses face issues… let's be honest).

Contrary to what you might read on the internet, there isn't a one-size-fits-all self-care checklist.

While self-care can definitely include:

Self-care also means showing up for yourself when no one else can. It means allowing yourself to snuggle in bed and cry after a massive break-up (we hate the guy too); it also means taking yourself to the spa after working really hard on a project. Self-care involves setting boundaries so that the next time your colleague texts you after office hours and asks you to work on the spreadsheet, you can politely decline. While social media glamorises self-care, remember, real self-care is usually not Instagram-worthy.

A fine lady understands, practices and encourages balance, and she does this knowing her boundaries won't always be perceived well by those wanting to get their own way.

We all want to feel more in control, and lead happier, healthier lives. This is the easiest way to do that.

Moral of the story:

Cut yourself some slack. You're doing your best.

Chapter 33

It's Okay to Mess Up

Perhaps you acted or spoke inappropriately in the heat of the moment because you were feeling emotionally unstable. Everyone has experienced it, and it is agonising.

And while we talk of mannerisms, etiquette also involves constantly being a work in progress. When you make a mistake, one of the most crucial things to do is to step back and see the problem from a different angle.

As natural as it is, don't go shaming yourself or focus on the error so much that it negatively affects your well-being or your ability to be yourself around others.

The thought of messing up is nearly horrifying in a world where we're expected to be flawless beings with ideal lives. You're human and mistakes are OK. More often than not, we overestimate a problem when it may not even be that big of a worry.

Chapter 34

Choosing the Right Career

In high school, most of us experience a wide range of emotions, and no amount of 'this will happen next' advice can adequately prepare you for your own experiences.

You don't have to set a direction for your entire life, so rest assured! People and their careers change over time (and we've seen this happen so very often).

All you have to do is start.

- Spend some time **reflecting on your hobbies and characteristics** to make sure the career ideas that are coming to you are a good fit.
- **Research different careers**. It may sound dull, but there is a heck of a lot of options. You owe it to yourself to at least skim job descriptions to see what stands out based on your perception of yourself and your gut feelings.
- And then **consider shadowing someone in that field**. When you do this, you gain experience through

internships or part-time jobs and you learn to network with professionals in the field.

- **Seek advice** from trusted friends, family or a career counsellor and **consider your financial and personal goals**.

Remember, finding the right career may take time, but it's worth the effort to find something that brings you happiness and satisfaction in the long run.

Don't be afraid to change direction, and please don't let societal pressure dictate your choice. Trust your instincts and find a career that aligns with your passions and allows you to live a fulfilling life.

Chapter 35

Complimenting in Style

In this Instagram-obsessed age, it's not uncommon to hear "you look beautiful!" This makes it more of a reason to give stronger, more meaningful compliments. Giving compliments that are more than just surface-level is a way of showing others that you truly see and appreciate them.

It's a simple but powerful tool that can be used to make others feel valued and appreciated.

A friend of mine recently started going to the gym and his physique is looking *damnnnnn fine*. He often gets "wow, you look amazing," but he says when he gets a "Wow, you're so dedicated and it shows," it makes him feel a lot better. People remember such compliments for life, and on the days they feel low, these can bring a smile to their faces.

The idea is to focus on the person's character traits,

achievements and skills. Instead of just saying "you look beautiful," try complimenting their kindness, intelligence or creativity. Consider the things that make the person unique and special and express appreciation for those qualities.

Of course, this works well only if you've known the person enough to compliment their traits or skills but remember, giving compliments that are more than just looks can have a huge impact on someone's self-esteem and boost their confidence, much more than we might even realise.

Chapter 36

Did it for the Gram!

Etiquette While Taking Photographs

Whether you're on your way to becoming an Instagram model or simply want to keep photographs as memories, it's important to understand not only how to take great photos but also how to do so in a respectful way.

I get what you're probably thinking – why would anyone follow photography etiquette? So extra…

Here's the thing – etiquette can be put to use in any situation, all it means is respecting and caring for others.

If someone asks you to take a photo of them, it's always nice to click a few rather than just one. Show off all the techniques you know – top angle, mid angle, low angle – this is your time to shine! Ask them to have a look at the images, and if they'd like more, please help them out with a nice smile.

I met a lady in Melbourne who asked me to take a picture of her and her boyfriend. Later she told me they were meeting after two years thanks to the long distance and how these photos are so important to them.

When taking photographs for yourself, it's important to consider the rights and privacy of others. This includes:

- Taking consent before clicking someone's picture.
- Avoid taking pictures of sensitive or confidential information.
- Respect cultural norms and traditions related to photography (e.g., avoid clicking pictures in places of worship, even if you don't follow the practice).
- If someone asks you not to click with them being in the surroundings, respect their comfort and personal space.
- When using a selfie stick, be careful not to hurt anyone.
- If you're travelling and getting clicked at a tourist attraction where there's a long queue, be quick and don't keep others waiting for long.

Chapter 37

Borrowing Clothes

So you have an important ball to attend to and nothing to wear – borrowing clothes is a wiser alternative to buying new clothes. Not only is it more cost-effective, but it is also a more sustainable way to stay fashionable.

Plus, it is an easy way to try new styles without committing to a purchase. However, it is important to have proper etiquette when borrowing from a friend.

Always ask for permission. Never assume. Before borrowing anything, it is important to get the approval of your friend. Pssst. Make sure you're close friends with this person; asking for clothes from acquaintances is just not okay.

Take good care of your clothes. Treat the borrowed clothes as if they were your own. Handle them with care and please return them in the same condition as you received them. Always wash, iron and fold them well before returning. A 'thank you' note is always appreciated.

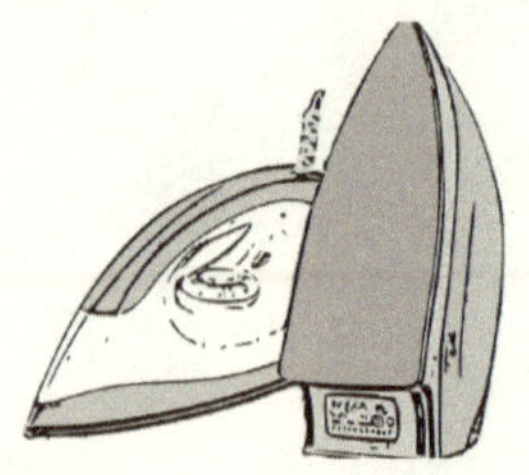

Be respectful. Do not borrow clothes without giving a proper reason, and never make fun of your friend's clothes.

Be prompt. Your friend might want to wear the dress she lent you and may feel embarrassed asking you to return it. Return the clothes as soon as you are done with them, don't keep them for an extended period.

Offer to repay the favour. If your friend is ever in need, offer to lend them something from your own wardrobe.

Now that you have your outfit for the ball sorted, remember: borrowing clothes from your gal-pals should be fun, not a cause of worry.

Chapter 38

Entering and Exiting a Car with Poise

A basic task for many, but an elegant task for a princess in training. Entering and exiting a car requires etiquette and mindfulness unless you want a disaster with people looking up at your skirt or down your top.

Whether you are getting in or out of a car in a personal or professional setting, it's important to follow some basic guidelines.

- To elegantly enter a car, bend your knees just a little and slide in from the backside. That means your hips touch the car seat first. Then lift your legs into the car and swing them to the front while keeping your knees firmly together.
- Never put your feet on the car's seat or dashboard.
- Unless it's a taxi, wait for the driver or person next to the door to open it for you.
- To exit, swing both legs out simultaneously, and only stand after both feet are on the ground.
- Take your belongings and thank the driver for the ride.

- Don't slam the door. Close it gently.
- If you're wearing anything with a low neckline, use your clutch as a cover while bending to get off the car.

Enter:

bum first, legs second

Exit:

legs first, bum second

Chapter 39

Gossiping and Keeping Secrets

Your parents are going to freak out over the tattoo that your sister just got. In a meeting with your boss, a co-worker claimed sole credit for a project you both worked on. You learn that your friend's ex is having a fling.

You're probably right if you think you would want to broadcast this kind of news. That's because we're human beings and part of what we do is share stuff. And in all honesty, who doesn't love a little drama?

Gossiping and keeping secrets involve a delicate balance that requires a good sense of judgement.

As long as people have trust in the person sharing the news about others (if it's you, only talk about others responsibly, leaving exaggeration at the door), talking about people and their lives can be harmless if done in a respectful way.

A poor gossiper, on the other hand, spreads rumours about others irresponsibly or with the intention of gaining an advantage. Being at the top of the social ladder is a strong addiction, unfortunately. Such people are not trusted, disliked and ultimately, socially avoided.

It is important to draw the line between the two and always keep in mind the potential consequences of what you are saying.

If someone tells you something and requests to keep it just to yourself, value it.

Remember, the more secrets you unveil, the more credibility you lose. Talk mindfully – when you speak more, you tend to spill information and spout what's on your mind.

We all admire royalty, and it's important to remember that royalty is often held in high regard because they are seen as dignified, reserved and, above all, discreet. Just like royals, we can choose to keep  grace and dignity by avoiding poor gossip and keeping secrets confidential.

Chapter 40

Choosing Your Signature Fragrance

Finding a fragrance you love can be challenging, regardless of whether you're a fragrance enthusiast or it's your first time investing in a good perfume. The only thing you can tell about any of the fragrances at first glance is how the bottle looks, which, of course, doesn't really tell you anything. Add to that an overbearing salesperson, who is often of no use at all.

A perfume you love might really become an extension of who you are, but what do you do when you're left to sniff from hundreds of bottles? How, then, do you find the one?

- Consider your daily life. Which fragrances do you already adore? Take into account the scent that you identify with your ideal lifestyle and mood.

- It goes without saying that trying the perfume on is the most important step. Take your time and try different fragrances to find the one that suits you best. Spray it on your wrist or elbow, which are areas of your body where your skin is naturally warm, to make the aroma really heat up and become more noticeable over time. The top notes of a perfume literally disappear within fifteen to thirty minutes, so be patient. It will take some time for the perfume to meld with your skin and unveil its true nature.

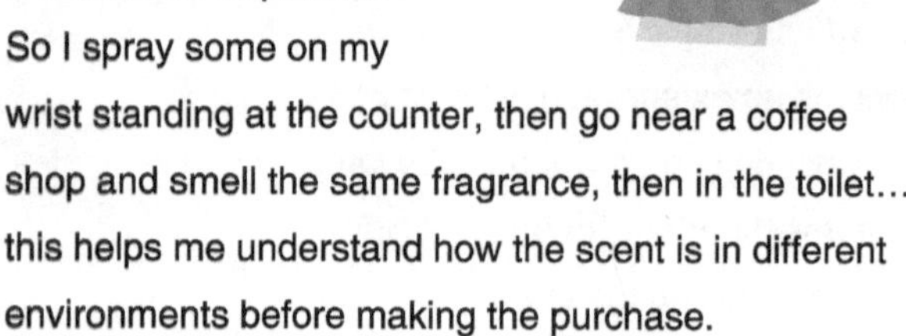

- Fragrances can be affected by heat, light, and even your own biological factors, dietary habits and hormonal levels. Every time I step into the airport duty-free stores, I'm tempted to buy a new bottle of perfume. So I spray some on my wrist standing at the counter, then go near a coffee shop and smell the same fragrance, then in the toilet… this helps me understand how the scent is in different environments before making the purchase.

- Having a signature fragrance makes a lasting impression and becomes part of your personal style, so it's important to choose one that reflects your personality.

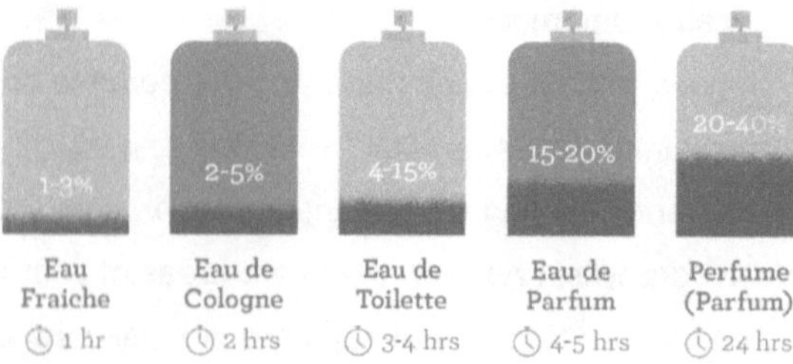

Fragrances – best kept a secret?

You toss down your credit card after smelling hundreds of essential oils and alcohols and testing them on every square inch of your body: wow, you've discovered your signature scent.

You adore it so much, you spritz it in your hair, on your neck, on your wrists, and directly on your chest. This scent is an expression of who you are. At the very least, this is something that makes you feel special in this vast, slowly inundating globe.

So just like your Instagram password, your phone's wallpaper, or your fancy (but very detailed) Starbucks order, nobody else should have access to the same thing, right?

Unless you feel okay (or excited) talking about your fragrance, a good way to divulge when someone asks what scent you're wearing is by saying:

"It's funny because the perfume was a gift and it reads something in French, but I didn't translate it yet" OR "I simply can't remember."

Chapter 41

Courtesy with Family

Are manners outdated? Nope! Should we follow good etiquette with family members? Absolutely!

What difference do these courtesies make? By establishing these, you're making everyone's expectations of one another apparent and providing them with practical suggestions for positively maintaining the environment that has the most personal influence on us all – our homes.

- **Greetings are common**: The daily comings and goings are acknowledged with greetings. By saying hello and goodbye, you are acknowledging the happenings of daily life – whether your sister is returning from work, your brother is leaving for a movie,  or your dad is leaving for his golf game. Reiterate to one another that the family is interested in the details of each other's lives.

- **Closed doors are respected:**
  They remind us of boundaries, like
  someone's time and privacy. Knock,
  say why you're there and wait for
  a response before opening the
  door. The first time I had seen kids
  telling their parents "get out of my
  room" was in Hollywood movies,
  and believe me, my jaw dropped. 

  It's just not common practice in India, but change starts
  with us. Make this a practice for yourself.
- **Turn small accomplishments into lasting memories**.
  We shouldn't reserve our fine cutlery and manners only
  for visitors. Value celebrating one another; it gives you
  yet another reason to host a party!
- **The inevitable heartaches and minor victories
  should receive proper attention** (like your sister's
  favourite tiffin box broke or your younger brother
  winning the class spelling bee). Our hearts require
  interaction, connection and care from one another just
  as much as our bodies require food.
- **Focused attention is essential**. Yes, there are huge
  issues that demand our attention every day, but when
  we do our work while listening to our dad or sister
  speak to us, we are just giving them a portion of
  ourselves. It's better to inform them that we want to
  give them our undivided attention, explain what we're
  doing, provide an estimated time of completion and ask
  if we can speak then.

- In many cultures, traditions like bowing down or saying 'namaste' are common ways of showing respect and honouring family members. If you are travelling and staying with a local family, a good way to build a connection is by learning about their customs.

- Remember that family members are the people who have been with us throughout our lives and have supported us in every step. They are the actual A-team! Yet, we often take them for granted. By being more mindful and conscious of how we treat our close and distant ones, we can strengthen our bonds and foster a more positive family dynamic.

Chapter 42

Making New Friends (& Starting All Over Again)

Most of us are blessed with great friends, but what happens when you move cities or change jobs?

When I went to college in London, I had to start all over again, and the process of making friends was daunting until I realised everyone, literally everyone, wants to make new friends. People are just nervous.

So I made the move – I spoke to my classmates who were from all over the world, and some of them became so close that I have a friend in almost every country now! It all happened just by saying a 'hello.'

The truth of the matter is, you may experience some level of nervousness when meeting new people. I did too, it's normal.

Understand your emotions the next time you try to make friends to see whether you have any anxiety, worry or uncertainty. Consider whether these thoughts are preventing your ability to make friends.

Pro tip: Being the popular girl at school may sound like fun, but it is a lot of unnecessary pressure and isn't really worth it. Release the stress to make a large number of friends and focus on developing one or two significant relationships.

While school may be an easier environment to make friends, new friendships develop throughout life, and most times we forget how to start over.

Do you prefer social situations when there are many people present, or do you prefer one-on-one interactions? Start by being a part of that environment.

Making a friend isn't enough, the real deal is to maintain the friendship. And this requires effort from both sides.

Communication: You don't need to talk every day, but keep in touch through calls, texts or visits. Update your friend about what's new with you, and listen to their life updates. This is even more important if your friend lives far away.

My friend Jagriti recently moved to Manila. While we may not talk every single day, we set monthly video call dates and update each other on everything that happened. Sometimes we even go overboard and make lists throughout the month so we don't forget the important stuff!

Take a genuine interest in their lives: This involves being a good listener and helping them out whenever you can.

Make quality time: Make plans to spend quality time together. Plan activities, or simply organise a stayover. Just as you would with family, give your bestie undivided attention.

Support each other: Be there through good and bad times. This has more power than anything else. An elegant lady knows when her friend needs her.

Chapter 43

Clarity is Everything

Having clarity in all areas of life is crucial for successful relationships, work and friendships. It helps in reducing confusion, improving communication and making good decisions.

Having clarity in relationships, whether it be family, friendships or romantic, helps set up healthy boundaries and clear communication. It allows us to understand each other's expectations and needs, leading to stronger, more fulfilling connections.

In work, clarity helps to set clear goals and expectations, leading to greater productivity and job satisfaction.

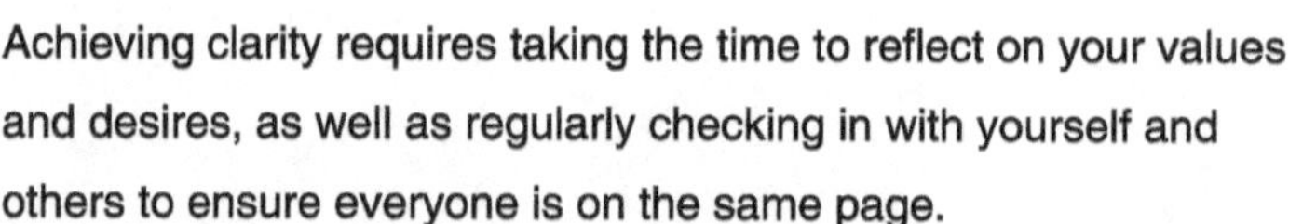

Achieving clarity requires taking the time to reflect on your values and desires, as well as regularly checking in with yourself and others to ensure everyone is on the same page.

Find what is important to you. What are your non-negotiables? If you value quality time with your boyfriend, and he's often on his phone when you meet, communicate that this is non-negotiable for you in a relationship. Similarly, if your parents keep talking to you while you're working from home, politely convey that you treat this time just like working from the office and that you'd like to set a clear boundary.

- If you're in the unofficial dating phase and you'd like to meet at least twice a week to get to know each other better, and if this is not open for debate, give the other person clarity and ask for it too.
- Set clear boundaries, communicate openly and honestly and regularly evaluate and reassess your own goals and values. By having clarity, you can lead a fulfilling life, with strong and meaningful connections.

Chapter 44

The 100% Rule

The phrase "99% is hard, 100% is easy" is one of the most motivating quotes I've heard.

Securing a perfect 100 is simple. Or, to put it another way (albeit more harshly), "99% is a bitch. 100% is a breeze," as Jack Canfield, best-selling author of *The Success Principles*, puts it.

Let's say you find it difficult to wake up at 7 am, so you snooze the alarm and wake up at nine. What if you repeatedly tell yourself you have no other option? You've got to wake up at 7 am and keep your feet on the ground, no matter what.

Similarly, if you skip gym days thinking you'll go tomorrow or the day after, you'll always give yourself leeway.

This is 99% effort, and this is hard.

As children, we have to go to school. There are no two ways about it. Even on the days, we feel lazy, we end up going. That's giving your 100%. 99% is just not an option.

Convincing yourself that it's got to be done is what the 100% rule is all about. And it's easier than it seems. Of course, to get better at something, you need to do it repeatedly and you need to choose just what you really want to focus on.

And here's why: focusing on everything is not necessary. If you give 100% to everything, you'll get exhausted and won't give your all to the thing that matters the most.

If you've been wanting to start journalling, dedicate yourself to writing for ten minutes, seven days a week. If you seriously take the time to plan out your first clothing line collection, you will absolutely be able to do it. However, if you only give it a 99% shot, it becomes easier to give excuses, avoid it and realise much later how much time you lost. Don't 99% it, give it 100%.

Chapter 45

Think Progress, Not Product

You've probably heard the phrase "strive for perfection" at some point. There is no greater grade in school than a perfect score, and there is no better position on your yearly performance review than being in the first place. Our culture's focus on perfection has historically inspired incredible inventions, but it has also caused some disastrous failures.

Perfectionism has its place – it promotes responsibility, accountability and quality. But if we get consumed in the end result, we forget to have fun along the way. Someone once asked me about my purpose in life. To me, progress is purpose. Progress, big or small, means I'm taking steps ahead.

My cousin is a home-baker. It started off as her passion and took off during the pandemic years. Over time, she got super busy with orders, so much so that she mentally and physically burnt out trying to be perfect. She took a break and didn't bake at all for about two months. This change in perspective allowed her to connect  back to her craft and to find joy in every step of the process.

Any YouTuber who tells you numbers don't matter is lying through their teeth. As unhealthy as it is, we all get consumed with numbers, and every creative person hits a point where they go, "Would this even get as many likes?"

Focusing that hard on the end result takes away the joy from the process. Worst case scenario: that video you thought would go viral probably got a hundred views, so what? If you at least enjoyed the process and put in more of your heart, you wouldn't feel so bad about it.

Focusing on the process allows one to learn and appreciate the effort put in, while the end result is just a reward. Embracing the process helps to reduce stress, increase motivation and overall lead to a more fulfilling experience.

Remember, it's not about the final outcome, it's about the progress made along the way. The journey is often more enjoyable than the destination.

Chapter 46

Create a Space You Love

Okay ladies, time to get your inner interior designer out! Creating a living space that reflects your personality, interests, and comforts can greatly improve your overall well-being and happiness. It is important to personalise your living space to reflect your style and create a welcoming atmosphere. Remember, your home reflects who you are, so make it a space you love.

- Find your style and aesthetic. Pinterest to the core!

- If you can get a designer on board, go ahead! If not, choose colours and materials that reflect your personality.

- De-clutter, organise your space and add personal touches like photos and art. Get them framed or showcase them as they are. You can even make a painting yourself to keep it more personalised.

- Make sure your furniture and decor are functional and comfortable. A pretty pink couch would look great, but if it's not comfy, you'd hardly ever want to sit on it.

- Consider lighting, both natural and artificial. Warm-toned lights are great for homes, whereas white lights are preferred for office spaces. If nothing else, get a pretty bedside lamp for yourself.
- Flowers always add a touch of freshness to the space. If you can care for them, opt for real flowers as opposed to fake ones.
- Regularly maintain and upgrade your space to keep it feeling fresh and loved.

Chapter 47

Going to the Movies

Truth be told, I can't live without watching movies, but let's face it: there is nothing more annoying than being seated and having to get up every time a latecomer wants to get to their seat in the row, or having the person next to you turn on their phone with full brightness, or someone going "I've seen this part… this happens next."

When people go to events, concerts, musicals or movies, they pay full price for a ticket, just like us, so it's important to be mindful of others around you. It's totally uncool to ruin these gatherings for other people.

Arrive on time to avoid disrupting the movie. If at all you arrive late, bend down while walking through rows to avoid blocking the view for others. Switch your phone to silent and avoid talking,

eating loudly or using your phone. If you need to use the restroom, do so during intermission or try to minimise the disruption to those around you. Respect the theatre's rules like

not bringing outside food or drinks. Follow seat arrangements and only sit on the seat you've bought the ticket for. And finally, once the movie is over, take responsibility for your own litter and dispose of it properly before leaving the theatre.

Pro tip: If you have a habit of sleeping and snoring while watching a movie, travelling or even in general (it's okay, a lot of people do), invest in an anti-snore device. This is especially important while travelling to ensure others have a pleasant experience. And if someone tells you that you snore, don't get offended. Life can get tiring, PLEASE make it easy for others to get some rest.

Chapter 48

Education: Your Passport to the World

Whether or not you're in school, studying certain subjects are important for personal and societal growth.

Every elegant lady should have a basic, if not in-depth, understanding of the following:

- English (to be able to converse fluently throughout the globe).
- Hindi or native language (comfortably read, write and speak in the language).
- French (this can be useful in situations such as dining at a restaurant, reading names of perfumes, etc.).
- History (understanding how events in the past made things the way they are today).
- Sport (of any kind, to develop physical fitness).
- Gemology (so you can separate the fake from the real and never be fooled).

- Styling (duh, this shouldn't even be a pointer – you need to look like a diva for important events).
- Martial arts (Judo, Karate, Kung Fu or any other kind of self-defence).
- Art/Dance/Music (of any kind, to develop your creative side).

And no, extra-curricular activities aren't just to meet cute boys (although we wouldn't mind some); colleges and companies also look at your overall persona. You can even choose to volunteer with an organisation you like. What most people don't realise is the people you meet while studying or volunteering will become tomorrow's Mark Zuckerberg or Elon Musk. So unless you want to be ignored by them at your school reunion, make sure you're being social.

Having a well-rounded education in these subjects will definitely improve your self-confidence, provide new interests and hobbies and offer practical knowledge for everyday life.

Pro tip: It's always a good idea to update your knowledge and stay curious to learn more. If you are done with formal education, there are many online websites that have certified courses (both, free and paid) in thousands of fields. This can even help if you took a career break, or want a field change. Find something that interests you and take the course to learn more!

Chapter 49

When a Guy Dumps You

Riding off into the sunset with prince charming seems great, except he dumped you, and there's probably nothing more you want than him coming back. I will take my role as the high school cupid, and tell you – everyone gets dumped. Even Jennifer Aniston.

While you wait for your heart to heal, and find a better, more charming prince to enter your life, give yourself time to process your emotions. It's normal to feel sad, angry or confused, but try not to let those feelings consume you.

Surround yourself with supportive friends and family members, engage in activities you enjoy and focus on self-care. Usually, relationships fall apart and there isn't one person who can be blamed. Do something, anything, to get your mind off the dude. And if at all you want to think of it, reflect on the experience and learn from it.

It'll hurt for a while, especially if this person posts stories while going out and carrying on with their life as usual; so, a good idea is to reduce social media contact (mute/unfollow/block – as deemed fit).

Cry truck loads, eat away all the ice cream you want, for as long as you want, and I promise you a day will come when you'll look back and think "Why did I cry so much?" In due time, it won't hurt as much as it used to and you'll meet a man who doesn't stick around for just one balayage.

I also promise the guy you always crushed on in seventh grade will tell you they've always wanted to talk to you.

Your happily-ever-after is waiting for you, just in time.

Chapter 50

Protecting Our Planet Starts with You

You want to make sure this planet and everything in it sticks around for a while, and even though it may seem like one person can't make a difference, the truth is that every small action we take adds up to a huge impact.

1. It starts with something as simple as turning off the lights when you leave a room, unplugging electronics and using energy-efficient products.

2. Minimise waste by reducing the number of resources you consume and recycling when possible. Carry a pretty reusable water bottle instead of buying single-use plastic.

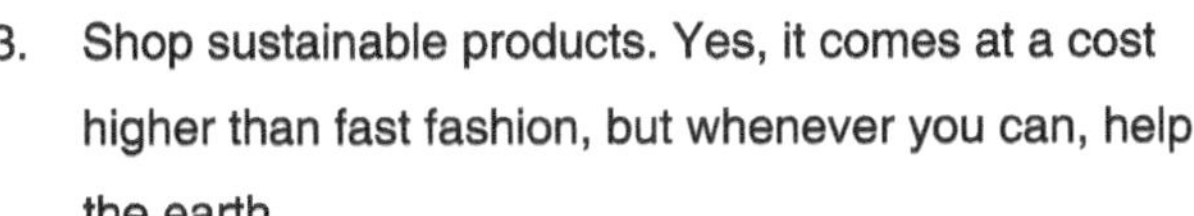

3. Shop sustainable products. Yes, it comes at a cost higher than fast fashion, but whenever you can, help the earth.

4.   I love long hot water baths. They feel almost therapeutic and are okay once in a while, but on a daily basis, reduce water usage by taking shorter showers, getting leaky faucets fixed, and using drought-resistant plants in landscaping, if possible.

5.   Support environmentally friendly policies. Educate yourself on environmental issues, vote for politicians who prioritise environmental protection, and support organisations working to protect the planet.

and finally

You're ready! The world is yours, really.

I hope you found this handbook of use. And as you now know, being elegant is more than just wearing expensive shoes and blow-drying your hair every day.

Keep in mind, manners matter and your kindness counts.

Texting your friend who had a break-up, making sure your friend reached home on time, talking to the new admission no one talks to – these are all acts of kindness and show you care.

But just because you are kind, don't let people tell you what to do – unless they actually want the best for you. Be assertive (politely) when you have to. A smile goes a long way. You don't have to fake it, but you want to keep those around you happy. If your best friend has a date on Valentine's and you don't, it's okay, elegant ladies don't go around crying and asking for pity. Go home, cry out loud into your pillow, and move on. Never let the whole wide world know what's bothering you (even if it is your crush not responding to your text after seeing your story).

And whether or not you have braces, green hair and tattoos over your arm, so long as you're happy, confident and yourself, you can be absolutely elegant.

May the lessons learnt in these pages inspire you to always approach the world with kindness and respect, and to be a queen in your own right. May these timeless principles guide you on your journey to becoming strong, confident and compassionate leaders. And remember, though there may not be enough thrones for all of us to reign as princesses, our etiquette can serve as the jewel that radiates our inner royalty, *making us truly crème de la crème.*

Live Long And Prosper.
CAFE

Acknowledgements

A big thank you to my mom, who taught me the value of respect, kindness and consideration for others, and because of whom I got all those 'well-groomed' good chits back in school. Thank you for setting such a wonderful example and for always encouraging me to do the same. I love you and I miss you every second of every day.

To Nanu, thank you for your teachings, and for putting up with my endless ramblings and the occasional writer's block. Thank you for your support (even on the days you didn't fully understand why on earth I wanted to write a book, but still encouraged me to go for it).

To Nani, who instilled in me from an early age the importance of good manners and polite behaviour; thank you for being my first and most important teacher in the art of etiquette.

To my friends, you all may be hopelessly crazy, but even if I got to choose all over again, I'd still choose to be with you.

To Tamiko, my instructor from finishing school, thank you for your invaluable insights and your commitment to studying the nuances and complexities of social behaviour.

To Candy, who has sat with me for countless hours as I
typed away, thank you for your quiet companionship and your
occasional paw on the keyboard (even if it did sometimes result in
a deleted paragraph or two).

To the coffee shop where I wrote most of this book, thank you for
your unwavering patience in fulfilling my often complicated frappé
orders.

To all those who have found their way to this book, thank you
for your interest in the art of etiquette. May these pages serve
as a guide and a source of inspiration as you navigate the social
landscape, and may you always remember that good manners
and respectful behaviour are forever going to be in.

And finally, to my online family, thank you for taking a chance on
me. I couldn't have done this without you!